MONEY
MANIA
AND
MORALS

ABINGDON PRESS new york—nashville

MONEY
MANIA
AND
MORALS

THE CHURCHES AND GAMBLING

Lycurgus M. Starkey, Jr.

MONEY, MANIA, AND MORALS

Copyright © 1964 by Abingdon Press

Library of Congress Catalog Card Number: 64-21177

SET UP, PRINTED, AND BOUND BY THE
PARTHENON   PRESS,   AT   NASHVILLE,
TENNESSEE, UNITED STATES OF AMERICA

To my two sons, Chris and Mark

PREFACE

Since World War II gambling has seen a considerable increase in the English-speaking world. Great Britain and Australia sponsor national lotteries and many other forms of government-supervised wagering. In the United States there has been a marked increase in gambling—90 per cent of it illegal according to one expert.

Several states have recognized and taxed various forms of gambling for the sake of government income. Hard-pressed state budget balancers, conscious of public resistance to increased taxes, look toward taxes on gambling as a voluntary form of state revenue acceptable with the people. Proposals for a national lottery are frequently heard. We are now experiencing a concerted effort to legalize and commend gambling as a national pastime.

At the same time greatly increased federal investigation and prosecution of organized crime has disclosed intricate ties between the underworld and gambling, both legal and illegal. Now organizations like Gambler's Anonymous have arisen to cope with the alarming rise of compulsive gambling.

A spate of books and popular magazine articles have treated the gambling crisis from various angles. All point to a problem area of American life which by volume and value-change does amount to a crisis.

Protestant and Orthodox Christians—with the assistance of the Jewish communities—have often been vocal in their opposition to gambling. Some of this opposition has been for the wrong reasons. The teaching of a negative, legalistic ethic in the churches has decreased in recent years; yet constructive teaching on gambling has seldom taken the place of the negative. Churchmen are for or against the practice with little awareness of the Christian issues involved. Churches have declared their positions and often left them buried in books of church law. Pamphlets have been published on the issue, but seldom with enough length to do justice to the subject. No thorough study of gambling from the biblical and theological perspective of the churches has been made. No attempt to compare and evaluate the positions of the churches and synagogues has been published. It is hoped the present volume will fulfill this need for churchmen who seek to understand and respond to the problems from a Christian perspective. Churches and synagogues, councils of churches, may find here new grounds of cooperation in fulfilling their citizenship responsibilities in the world. Public officials faced with gambling legislation will also have here a guide to the teachings of the churches.

In the preparation of this volume I am indebted to Roger Burgess, Associate-General Secretary, and Leighton E. Harrell, Chaplain, Division of Temperance and General Welfare, Board of Christian Social Concerns of The Methodist Church. Harold Bassett, my student research assistant, has collected materials, criticized the manuscript, and prepared the index. Mrs. Romaine Barber has ably served the project as typist. To these and many others I am deeply grateful.

Now to the thought, the word, the deed.

> Come, Holy Spirit, come.
> . . . until
> Every thought we think, and
> Every word we say, and
> Every deed we do
> Be to thy glory and
> For the coming of thy kingdom;
> Through Jesus Christ our Lord. Amen.

—LYCURGUS M. STARKEY, JR.

CONTENTS

CONTENTS

1

THE ITCH FOR PLAY[1]

The boys in the office work up a football pool. The P.T.A. operates a cakewalk at the school bazaar. The kids sell chances on a television set at the church fair. The bookie takes two-dollar bets in the Pentagon and at the local newsstand. The candy store operates punchboards and pinball machines with payoffs for the grade-school crowd. Mother plunks down her dollar for the bridge game prizes. Dad continues to play the horses in spite of bankruptcy.

In a small Midwestern town a plumber considered one of the best gets involved in a series of high-stake poker games. In an increasingly desperate attempt to recoup his losses he keeps playing.

[1] Title of a recent book on gambling by L. J. Ludovici (London: Jarrolds Publishers, Ltd.).

Finally he forfeits his once thriving business through neglect and debt. "I can't stop myself," he tells a friend. "I've got to get even."

A state governor, along with other socially prominent leaders, spends an evening on a gambling ship outside the three-mile limit. It's all for charity. "These wealthy people can afford to lose for a good cause," the argument goes. Meanwhile the great mass of low-income folk within the governor's three-mile limit clamor for legalizing a neighborhood bookie where they can conveniently place their bets.

Harold Smith, Sr., the proprietor of Harold's Club in Reno, Nevada, said, "I love money, whiskey and women—and I don't care who knows it. . . . I love my gambling fraternity. Compared to some politicians and bankers, we have true values and concepts. Socrates said, 'You don't want to hear the truth!' Well, I am the guy who throws the truth at the people." [2]

Jimmy Breslin, a Roman Catholic layman, set forth his reasons why a citizen has the right to gamble and why anti-gamblers should keep their mouths shut! He said:

There is nothing morally wrong with gambling, and everybody ought to have the right to bet. But outmoded laws and blue-nose thinkers infringe upon our right to gamble. Legal wagers are separated from illegal ones merely by the technique of placing the bet. The bet made on the street corner is unlawful while the one at the track has the blessing and encouragement of the state.

This distinction infuriates me. . . .

The important thing is, all of this is up to me. I decide whether or not I am going to gamble . . . nobody, whether he is a politician or a clergyman or a policeman, should tell me I cannot. [3]

[2] *Look* (March 12, 1963), pp. 28-29.
[3] *Saturday Evening Post* (January 5-January 12, 1963), p. 12.

Some wager privately; some wager legally; some wager illegally; some wager addictively. All in all a majority of adult Americans spend an estimated 50,000,000,000 dollars a year on gambling.[4] In some states this means the public pays out more for gambling than for groceries. On a national level, by some estimates, Americans spend more on gambling than on national defense. In 1962 Britons spent twice as much on gambling as to support the British navy.

A DEFINITION OF GAMBLING

For most people today gambling means betting on such sports events as horse races, playing poker, putting coins into slot machines, or taking part in lotteries. Gambling is frequently associated with leisure-time amusement and the suave sophistication of television's Mr. Lucky. "Characteristically American" say tourists from other countries, who insist on seeing the neon lights, rich hotels, smart clubs, and wide-open gambling casinos of Las Vegas and Reno.

Legal accuracy would distinguish three requirements for any activity to be defined as gambling.[5] First, there must be a prize or payoff in money or merchandise. Secondly, the awarding of this prize must be largely by chance, though skill may be involved in some games. In the third place, eligibility for the prize must depend not only upon the chance taken, but on a necessary payment of consideration in either money or merchandise by the player. There is no consideration or a fee put up in a private wager; yet the wagerer does in fact offer the money or goods he wagers as a fee. Indeed, the money may be held by a third party.

[4] See *Life* (June 19, 1950), pp. 96-121; *The Nation* (October 22, 1960), p. 311; *Look, op. cit.,* p. 26.

[5] Virgil W. Peterson, "Obstacles to Enforcement of Gambling Laws," *The Annals of the American Academy of Political and Social Science* (May, 1950), p. 5. See Francis Emmett Williams, *Lotteries, Laws and Morals* (New York: Vantage Press, 1958).

SPECIFIC FORMS OF GAMBLING

These three characteristics of gambling may be seen in the following:

1. *Betting on horse and dog racing.* The principal form of gambling in the English-speaking countries has grown in popularity since the invention of the pari-mutuel machine in 1860. Twice as many people go to horse races as to ball games. In pari-mutuel betting winners generally have a mutual share in the winning stake forfeited by the losers. All bets are registered on an automatic "totalizator" machine to compute the official odds and allow for the track's and the state's percentages. These percentages take the cream off the top of all money wagered so as inevitably to stack the odds against the bettor. Approximately 3,600,000,000 dollars was bet last year at over 130 horse tracks in 24 states.[6] Daily betting averaged about $76.20 per person in attendance at United States tracks in 1961.[7] The illegal off-track take is estimated to be several times as much.

Illegal betting with a "bookie" appears to be more attractive because no percentage of the winnings must be paid the state or the track. The odds against the bettor may be even greater, however, since the off-track bookies limit payoff, according to Ernest E. Blanche, a former chief statistician for the United States Army Logistics Division.[8]

2. *Betting on sports events.* Much of this kind of gambling is still merely between friends, but an increasing amount is handled by

[6] *Time,* "How to Raise Money Without Really Trying" (April 5, 1963), p. 29.

[7] *Look, op. cit.,* p. 26.

[8] *You Can't Win: Facts and Fallacies About Gambling* (Washington, D.C.: Public Affairs Press, 1949), pp. 55-56.

a vast network of illegal bookies and parlay card salesmen. These syndicated professionals now handle about half the nation's sports betting, according to John Scarne, a noted authority on gambling.[9] Betting runs high on such sports events as baseball, college and pro football, prize fights, basketball, and hockey. Fifty to sixty million dollars changes hands on a typical fall weekend over professional and college football games. Forty or fifty million dollars bet on summer baseball is illegally handled by bookies.[10] Parlay bosses keep eighty cents of every dollar bet with them according to the Senate subcommittee on gambling and organized crime.[11]

Some of this betting in the United States and Great Britain is on a pool basis. The bettor's task is to name the winning teams in three or more games. In baseball he must predict the number of hits or runs a named team will make during the week. Payoffs on actual odds[12] of 15 or 16 to 1 amount to about 3 to 1, whereas actual odds of 300 to 1 may deliver a pay off of 100 to 1. The difference goes for promotion expenses and the promoter's sure profit. Pool betting was legalized subject to government inspection by Great Britain in 1954.[13]

3. *Lotteries, sweepstakes, and bingo.* One of the oldest forms of gambling, the lottery is an arrangement for the distribution of prizes by chance among persons purchasing tickets. Slips, or lots, bearing the same numbers as the tickets and representing either prizes or blanks are drawn from a wheel. From the income realized by the sale of the tickets the lottery proprietor withdraws arbitrary sums for promotional expenses and profits; the remainder is re-

---

[9] John Scarne, *Scarne's Complete Guide to Gambling* (New York: Simon and Schuster, Inc., 1961), pp. 2-3.
[10] *Newsweek*, "The Mania to Bet on Sports" (June 6, 1960), p. 75.
[11] *Look, op. cit.*, p. 27.
[12] Odds or mathematical probabilities of winning.
[13] *Encyclopaedia Britannica*, IX, 999.

turned in prizes to the lucky ticket holders. Attractive to those of moderate income because of the huge prizes compared to the small investment, lotteries offer actual odds against winning that are fantastic. For example, 40 per cent or less of the proceeds are earmarked for prizes in the well-publicized Irish Sweepstakes.[14] The amount of profit for promoters in this sweepstake is not published, but estimates indicate only 17½ per cent of the proceeds actually go to the hospitals of Ireland which front for the operation. In 1954 about 27,000,000 dollars was staked in the three drawings of the Irish Sweepstakes.

The sweepstake differs slightly from the straight lottery. The drawing is for tickets naming horses which compete in a race. In the Irish sweeps the ticket buyer's chance of winning the top award is 1 in 305,000; of drawing a horse that places first, second, or third, 1 to 101,666, and of even drawing a horse listed as a possible starter, 1 in 3,470.

Sweepstakes and lottery tickets or payments for them, may not legally be sent through the United States mails, but the tickets are smuggled into this country and their sale supervised in spite of all the post office law-enforcement officers can do.

The largest legal lottery operation in United States history was the Louisiana Lottery Company. For twenty-five years this ruthless gambling operation controlled Louisiana politics and tried to enforce its will upon a national presidential election. At the peak of its success its income was 30,000,000 dollars annually. It was eliminated by an angry Louisiana electorate in 1890.

In the spring of 1963 the state of New Hampshire created the first legal lottery in the United States since the dismal demise of the Louisiana Lottery. In 1964 citizens will be able to risk three

[14] Gordon H. Cole and Sidney Margolius, "When You Gamble—It's More Than Your Money" Public Affairs Committee, Inc. (January, 1964), p. 10.

dollars for a sweepstakes ticket twice a year. Prizes will depend on the number of tickets sold. The state's percentage for educational purposes is not yet known.

Another form of lottery promotion, legal in some states, is bingo. States with legalized bingo include New York, New Jersey, Nevada, Vermont, Connecticut, Rhode Island, New Hampshire, Minnesota, Maine, Maryland, and Alaska. Seventeen million play annually. Players compete with each other to first line up a winning series of five random numbers on a card purchased for play from the bingo parlor. Numbers from 16-75, as in any lottery, are drawn from a wheel or its equivalent. In illegal bingo—such as is played at many carnivals for community charity—promoters are believed to return only 50 per cent of the proceeds in prizes. The New York State Bingo Control Commission indicates that even legal operators retain 34 per cent of the proceeds. The odds at best are 3 to 2; 66 cents back for the average dollar.[15] In New York State alone over 40,000,000 dollars net profit was gained by sponsoring organizations in the first four years of state control. This meant that an estimated 80,000,000 dollars went somewhere other than to the sponsoring groups. These sponsors usually are veterans' and fraternal organizations, and some churches.

4. *The policy or numbers game.* Often called the poor man's lottery, policy is illegal throughout the United States and is especially susceptible to graft. Amounts as small as a dime will purchase a three number combination, anything from 000 to 999. The winning number each day is taken from some officially published figure such as the last three digits of the United States Treasury balance, a local clearinghouse balance, or a racetrack parimutuel total. Some newspapers assist by publishing such data daily. An estimated 5,000,000,000 dollars is bet on the numbers each year

[15] *Ibid.,* p. 8.

in the United States.[16] Theoretically a winner should receive a return of 1,000 to 1 for each ticket, but the policy operator may pay only 500 or even 400 to 1.

5. *Dice and card games.* Frequently such games are played among friends, at times without stakes. In using these many dice and card games for gambling, players wager on the outcome of a game. In England the courts have held poker and occasionally contract bridge to be games of chance. In the United States most courts consider contract bridge to be a game of skill and hence not subject to the anti-gambling laws. Poker has been ruled in both categories. Scarne has credited the ladies' bridge game for stakes with introducing women to the playing of poker, blackjack, and other card games for money.[17] These games and many others may be found under legal and illegal auspices in all parts of the country.

According to the *Encyclopaedia Britannica,* a professional survey in 1944 revealed that there were gambling houses located within a thirty-mile radius of any point in the United States. This excepted only a few sparsely settled sections. In most gambling casinos players may not bet among themselves, but only against the house. The house often maintains an exorbitant mathematical advantage. Honestly operated, the gambling casino may take as little as 6 per cent of the amount wagered at blackjack or twenty-one. Bank craps give gamblers the best odds. Shooters play against a handicap of only 1.414 percent. The legitimacy of professionally operated dice and card games cannot be taken for granted, however. Gambling supply houses openly advertise an amazing assortment of crooked paraphernalia—loaded dice, magnetized tables, marked cards, and other hustling devices.

6. *Slot machines and "payoff" pinball machines.* Slot machines

[16] Scarne, *op. cit.,* p. 164.
[17] *Ibid.,* p. 8.

probably provide over 600,000,000 dollars profit annually for slot operators and the poorest odds for players. In playing these machines one inserts a coin in a slot, thus setting the machine in motion. The player gets back from two to two hundred coins if a winning combination shows. Machines can be adjusted to return any amount—generally 60 to 90 per cent—and keep whatever the proprietor wants.[18] Even when the machine is adjusted for a relatively generous payment the jackpot combination appears only once in about four thousand spins. Slot machines are illegal in all but five states, and Maryland has recently moved to eliminate them gradually because of their depressive effect upon the economy and their associations with the underworld.

Pinball has been called the little brother of the slot machine by Ernest Blanche. He estimated over a million pinball machines in operation in the United States, with a total annual "take" of over 2,000,000,000 dollars.[19] Honest machines operate on a basis of 60 per cent for the house and 40 per cent for the player. Instructions on "gimmicking" the machine are furnished by the supplier, however, so the operator can have an 80-20 take if he wishes. Pinball playing clearly becomes gambling and illegal when storekeepers exchange free games won for cash or merchandise.

PSEUDO-GAMBLING

In addition to these games legally defined as gambling there are many other practices in American life which may be termed pseudo-gambling. The multiplicity of give-away gimmicks to lure the consumer in the marketplace have contributed to the thirst for easy money gained without regard to service performed. Hardly anyone,

[18] See *Gambling Devices Within the United States,* a research project of the Maryland Crime Investigating Committee.

[19] See "Pin-ball: 'Little Brother' of the Slot Machines," *Concern* (April 1, 1963), pp. 3 ff.

especially if they have young children, ever buys breakfast food for the cereal in the box. Rather we buy frontier villages, cutouts, and pinups, and generally some cereal is thrown in on the side. Every housewife can get a practically free stainless steel teaspoon by sending the coupons from seventy-five boxes of Betty Biddy products plus a thin dime.

The "Peanuts" comic strip for December 5, 1963, shows Linus writing to Santa Claus. He asks Lucy, "How do you suppose Santa Claus can afford to give away all those toys?" "Promotion," says Lucy. "Don't kid yourself. . . . Everything these days is promotion! I'll bet if the truth were brought out, you'd find that he's being financed by some big eastern chain!"

In 1956 the quiz show sponsors passed out 5,000,000 dollars worth of easy money. They succeeded in drawing the interest and identification of a vast throng of the video viewing public. Subsequently it was revealed that these shows were rigged from sponsor to contestant for the purpose of duping the public's interest in the sponsor's product. Moral compromise was observed on all sides. Many Americans who might have been expected to be deeply concerned hardly seemed to care.

Many people have become professional contest participants. These contests are not strictly gambling if the winner is determined on the basis of skill and not chance. Contests which required soap wrappers as entry fees were, with the movie "bank" night, regarded in most states as lotteries. Then the soap companies required that the wrappers be accompanied by a statement of "twenty-five words or less"—in case of the bank night an admission fee and attendance were not required to win.

The *Wall Street Journal* for March 27, 1963, headlined "Games Offering Cash Join Trading Stamps As Supermarket Lure." Thousands of supermarkets play "Spell C-a-s-h" and "Split the Dollar."

"Super Poker," a modified version of five-card draw, has boosted sales in some stores as much as 10 per cent. "Women are like everyone else," says an advertising manager for Grand Union Company. "They like to gamble. And the fact that they can do it without investing their own funds makes it all the more appealing." Stores generally avoid gambling litigation by allowing shoppers to participate whether or not they buy anything. These merchandizing lures do not require a consideration from the patron. The elements of a prize determined by chance are present, however.

Herbert A. Bloch, professor of sociology and anthropology at Brooklyn College of the City University of New York, points to some forms of speculation in the stock market as pseudo-gambling. He speaks not of the trading necessary to sound investment, but of the sheerly speculative quick turnover maintained on a dubious margin. On the occasion of the 1962 collapse in the market the Board of Governors of the Stock Exchange argued that such speculation endangers the economy and "constitutes a particularly sinister form of 'making book' with partially solvent claims." [20]

Though the letter of the law has been met, many of these operations may be termed pseudo-gambling. The influence of such practices upon the integrity and initiative as well as the economy of our people is certainly related to the motivations which sustain gambling in our culture. Chapters 3 and 4 will give more consideration to the motivations of gambling.

WHAT GAMBLING IS NOT

1. *Gambling is not a necessary risk of life.* "All life is a gamble," some say—the stock market, farming, raising a family, even faith, according to some theologians. Why should the wagering of money

---

[20] "How to Control Gambling," *Concern* (May 15, 1963), p. 5.

in a game of chance be considered differently than the investing of time, money, and effort in the chancy game of life?

Life does have its normal risks which one must accept with faith and courage. These normal risks are in no sense equivalent to the risks in a game of chance. Gambling devises artificial risks in the hope of excessive gain far beyond what the investment of time, money, or skill would justify. In gambling the chance is unrelated to any creative effort called for by the farmer or the stockbroker in the responsible investment of his mental, monetary, and physical funds.

Economists long ago distinguished between gambling and other forms of risk-taking, asserted Arnold E. Barrett, associate professor of economics at the University of Alabama:

Those who define the natural risks of life as gambles are guilty of "fuzzy" thinking at best, careless or deceptive thinking at worst. . . .

The professional speculator does not gamble in any sense of the word. To be sure he pits his skill and knowledge against the inexorable forces of the market as he tries to guess which way the market will move. And he must be right more often than he is wrong in order to succeed in his calling. But in every case of his buying and selling he is undertaking risks that someone else would have to take if he did not do so. . . .

The insurance business is not a betting business, as some assert. It is simply a sophisticated and professional method for sharing risks of certain and uncertain events.

The intent of insurance is to make up for losses rather than to create them. "It would seem," Barrett continued, "that those who create and take artificial risks which produce nothing of value are simply withdrawing from that reality of life where the truly challenging and productive risks abound." [21] At the gaming table money changes hands according to the luck of the persons involved. Results depend not upon effort or ingenuity but on the turn of a wheel, the throw of dice, the odds on a race, or the drawing of a number. Gambling is not a necessary risk of life.

2. *Gambling is not instinctive with human beings.* In many times and places men have been able to bet their shirts and lose their pants. Why fight what seems to be human nature? Let us rather control gambling by strict legislation and governmental supervision. Then taxes on gambling can go to the state and be returned to the people in services. So the argument goes.

To this ancient plea for legalized vice—respectability by recognition—we must answer that gambling is not instinctive to man. The Massachusetts Crime Commission has shown that bookmaking, the most important racket of the underworld, did not even exist as a crime problem worthy of mention until pari-mutuels were legalized. Legalized pari-mutuel betting has led to a growth in gambling on the track, and illegally off the track as well. Gambling, said award-winning reporter Fred J. Cook, "is an acquired habit, and nothing shows this more clearly than the manner in which it was stimulated and grew in Massachusetts under the opening wedge of the pari-mutuel system. . . . As the Massachusetts commission said bluntly, 'There has not always been gambling with organized racketeers on a scale which amounts to a state of lawlessness in an entire society and there need not be.' " [22]

Recent British experience seems to confirm this Massachusetts Crime Commission position concerning the learned character of gambling. According to the *New York Times* of April 4, 1963,

[21] "Gambling, Economics, and Morality," *Christianity Today* (June 21, 1963), pp. 38, 39.
[22] "Gambling, Inc.," *The Nation* (October 22, 1960), p. 304.

"The rate of gambling in Britain has reached a new record, alarming the churches and disconcerting the Government." The government plans new taxes on gambling to drain off more of the easy money. The total on gambling for 1962 in Great Britain (not including the illegal and private club receipts) reached 853,300,000 pounds (2,389,240,000 dollars) which represents an increase of 90,868,000 pounds (254,430,400 dollars) over the estimate of the previous year (1961). The open legalization of gambling in Britain has not regularized an instinct; it has taught Britons the gambling habit.

The *Encyclopaedia Britannica* confirmed this observation of recent British and American history: "Gambling has sometimes been called instinctive in man, but this view is not widely held. It is more usual to consider gambling unnatural, though an inevitable concomitant of man's basic cultural patterns." [23] Gambling is more prevalent among hunting, pastoral, military and mercantile societies than peasants who live close to the soil and must work hard to acquire substance.[24] "It has been discovered that the use of leisure becomes especially congenial to gambling of all sorts, public and private, when work is sharply separated from leisure and where work loses its utility as a calling, is highly routine and mechanized and characterized by drudgery and boredom." [25] All of this points to the culturally influenced, learned character of gambling. Human beings may have a desire for gain, a desire for excitement, an instinct of combativeness. These drives may be directed to contribute to the well-being of the individual and society, or they may be misdirected toward gambling. Gambling is not instinctive with human beings.

[23] "Gambling and Betting," IX. See also reference to anthropological discoveries of nongambling peoples in Chapter 2 of this book.

[24] *Encyclopedia of Religion and Ethics*, VI, 163.

[25] Bloch, *op. cit.*, p. 4.

3. *Gambling is not merely amusement.* More than for pleasure, men gamble for profit. The motivations for gambling are not simple, however. The great seventeenth-century French theologian and mathematician, Blaise Pascal, said in his *Pensées:*

> Such and such a man spends his life playing everyday for a small stake. Give him every morning the money that he may gain during the day, on condition that he does not play—you will make him unhappy. It will perhaps be said that what he seeks is the amusement of play, not gain. Let him play then for nothing: he will lose his interest and be wearied.

The real motive for violation of the anti-gambling laws is not the desire for pleasure, but the avarice for easy money, says Virgil Peterson, Executive Director of the Chicago Crime Commission. He quotes the well-known columnist Herb Graffis: "Churches and charitable organizations run illegal gambling because that's the sure way of getting money for holy causes from people who otherwise wouldn't contribute if the Almighty pushed a .45 at them." [26] Gambling is always based on a desire to get something for nothing, to take something away from someone else while giving nothing in return. In addition to greed, Pascal intimates a certain fatal fascination, like that of the moth for the candle, in gaming. There is a thrill, a fever, an excitement, that appeals to a peculiar personality need in ways even the gamblers do not recognize. But avarice is at the heart of the fascination. Take away the greed for gain, as Pascal suggests, and the thrill is gone out of it.

4. *Gambling is not a way to acquire wealth. You Can't Win* is the title of a book on gambling by statistician Ernest Blanche, a student of gambling for twenty-five years. We have already seen

[26] "A History of Legalized Gambling," *Annals of the American Academy of Political and Social Science* (May, 1950), p. 13.

the odds stacked against the player in the various professionally operated gambling enterprizes. The margin the professional has against you ranges from 15 to 60 per cent. This is true even at the legal race tracks of the country. The track and the government between them take as much as 15 to 22 per cent out of the pot before the winnings are divided. If you want to make money in horse racing don't gamble; own a race track. Elbert Hubbard cynically remarked, "The only man who makes money following the races is the one who does so with a broom and shovel."

It is common knowledge in gambling circles that big gamblers die poor. The professional doesn't gamble. He just takes an assured profit out of the money you want to lose. In the numbers or policy game a winner should take home 1,000 to 1, but the operators usually pay only 600 to 1 and after deducting the 10 per cent of the winnings. The runner (salesman) customarily collects only 540 to 1. Thus of 1,000 bettors who pay one dollar each, or a total of 1,000 dollars, one will win, on the average, 540 dollars. Modern probability theory shows that if the gambler continues to play he will always lose. "Mathematicians have shown that the chances of loss become greater and greater as the gambler continues to play and the resources of the house increase compared to those of the gambler." [27]

You can't win; the operator can't lose. No wonder the customer is generally termed a "sucker," the loser the hero in most gambling stories and jokes.

"Thus, the anecdote of the faro addict who rushed into his home in midafternoon, after being busted. He ordered his wife to heat the last can of beans in the house.

"Why? It's too early for supper," she said.

[27] *Kansas City Star*, "Science Service, Inc." (September 17, 1963), p. 16.

"Heat the beans," he insisted. "After I eat, I'm hocking the stove and going back to play!" [28]

CONCLUSION

So this is the itch for play in America. At least 55 per cent of the American adult public [29] contributes a possible 50,000,000,000 dollars to the big, big business of gambling. Men favor betting on races and sports events. Women prefer bingo and the numbers game. Wealthy women who gamble have a fondness for roulette. The children learn to gamble from their parents—on sporting events, card games, dice, slot machines, punchboards, pinball, and other games. A children's game called "One-armed Bandit," based on slot machines and played with simulated silver dollars, was introduced for Christmas giving in 1963.

Gambling is on the increase in the United States; it has doubled in recent years according to Scarne. He points out that both the number of paid admissions to racetracks and the total sum bet doubled from 1949 to 1960, and that revenues reported by Nevada's legal gambling establishments increased five times in that period.[30]

Such a multibillion dollar industry pours profits into the coffers of the professional operators. More than the 5,000,000,000 dollars a year we spend for private education and research, more than all we devote to welfare and religious activities (*less* than 5,000,000,-000), more than the combined profits of the one hundred largest United States manufacturing corporations (a little in excess of 8,000,000,000 dollars annually)—more than for any one of these

[28] *Look, op. cit.,* p. 27.
[29] See Gallup Poll results for 1950 in George Gallup, "More Than Half of Us Gamble," *Gambling in America,* edited by H. L. Marx, Jr. (New York: H. W. Wilson Company, 1952), pp. 25 ff. Scarne (*op. cit.,* p. 1) estimates that 70 per cent of the adult population—86,000,000 Americans—wager 500,000,000,000 dollars annually, 98 per cent of it illegally.
[30] *Ibid.,* p. 3.

the American people devotedly give 9 to 10,000,000,000 dollars profit annually to the gambling industry. And in return we get precisely what we deserve.

As we have seen, gambling refers to games in which a consideration of money or merchandise is offered by the gambler for a prize, the awarding of which is determined largely by chance. Gamblers don't gamble. As distinguished from the ordinary risks and hazards of life which contribute to the economic, mental, moral, spiritual, and social well-being of the nation, gambling may be further defined as an artificial risk or hazard for hope of excessive gain, far beyond what the investment of time, money, or skill would justify. Gambling is motivated by the greed for gain in the operator and the gambler rather than the desire for amusement. It is not instinctive but an acquired habit. It is not a dependable way to acquire wealth. It produces no economic value for the community, and the few who do win do so at the expense of the many.

2

A HISTORICAL SKETCH

There are those who would associate anti-gambling legislation with a rather recent American puritanism. They would see the social problems in gambling as due to the attempt of religious groups to legislate their own repressive moral positions. Supposedly gambling was never a problem or a subject of prohibitory legislation earlier than the seventeenth century. A historical sketch of gambling will disclose the truth of the matter.

THE ORIGINS OF GAMBLING

1. *Early religious associations.* Imagine yourself in a campfire circle of primitive men sometime near the dawn of recorded history. The tribe is preparing for a seasonal hunt for winter provisions. The shaman, a combination of priest, seer, and medical man, performs his mysteries. He would bring the blessings of the spirits

upon the hunters and their efforts. To determine the day of departure and the direction of the hunt he takes the knuckle bones of a goat and throws them onto the smoothed earth. These bones from the hind feet of a goat are differently marked on four sides. Their fall is directed by the spirits, and their message is read for the hunt by the shaman.

Gambling is as old as man himself and predates civilization. It probably began as a religious ritual for divining the future, for ascertaining the will of the gods. Bones, sticks, arrows, lots, were shuffled, thrown, and chosen by the tribal seer. They disclosed the mystery of the future and won supernatural counsel. Early American Indians believed their gods were the originators of their gambling games with colored stones. The gods sponsored their outcome.[1]

Divination by appeal to chance is frequently found in the Old Testament. In the midst of the storm the sailors from Joppa to Tarshish cast lots to discern the blame for the wrath of heaven. The lot fell upon Jonah, and he was cast into the sea to appease the deity (Jonah 1:7). By lot Aaron determined the goats for the sacrifice and the scapegoat (Lev. 16:7-10). The promised land was divided among the twelve tribes by lot (Num. 26:55). Even kings and priests were chosen in this manner of discerning the will of God (I Sam. 10:20-21; I Chr. 24:5; 25:8; 26:13). Indeed the Urim and Thummim carried in the Ark of the Covenant were probably like dice. Marked so as to indicate a "yes" or "no" answer, they were "cast before the Lord our God." The Jews believed the decision was wholly from God—hence there was neither magic nor witchcraft to them. Even in the New Testament there is indication that Matthias, the twelfth disciple, successor to Judas, was chosen by the "lot" (Acts 1:26).

[1] Henry Chafetz, *Play the Devil* (New York: Clarkson N. Potter, Inc., Publisher, 1960), p. 7.

Generally, this practice in Israel died out with the appearance of the prophets. Through them God could disclose his will far more eloquently than by divination.

2. *Primitive players.* The step between divination and gambling, the use of divination for private gain, is a short one. The greed that gambles goes back a long way in the history of man and is found in most every country. Ur of the Chaldees, excavated by Sir Leonard Woolley, has revealed a gaming board from about 2000 B.C. The Chinese, inveterate gamblers to this day, have records of gambling games from about 2300 B.C. Chinese gamblers were reputed to have staked their hands and, losing them, cut them off. The Greeks of Homer's day used the knuckle bones, which were also used in gambling as far back as the twenty-eighth dynasty in Egypt. Originally they were marked on four sides. Then the six-sided marking of dice was introduced, probably from Arabia. Early references from Indian literature reveal the ardent love of dice playing and some of the evil consequences of the same. The Hindu Code of Manu, written about 100 A.D. advised: "Let the King forbid gambling and betting in his kingdom, for these are vices that destroy the kingdoms of princes."

Like the early Chinese, primitive peoples to this day are willing to put up personal stakes in the losing desperation of the game. Gamesters of the Sarpoe tribe in Liberia wager on a top game played on a cloth-covered basket. They are known to mortgage even their wives and their daughters to pay their gambling debts. Chafetz tells of a similar incident among the Indians of the Western United States.

Even legalized gambling dates back to the pre-Christian era. From 321-296 B.C., during the reign of Chandragupta in India, a department of the state controlled gambling. Taxes on gambling houses replenished the state treasury. The supervision and taxation of prostitution was also maintained by Chandragupta.[2]

Always in Israel a distinct difference was made between divining the will of God and gambling. Gambling for private gain does not seem to have appeared in Israel until late. The agricultural Jews picked up gambling from the commercial-military culture of the Babylonians during the exile. In the Book of Isaiah after the exile God condemns the Israelites for gambling:

> Ye who have forsaken the Eternal,
> ye who ignore his sacred hill,
> spreading tables to Good Luck,
> pouring libations to Fate. . . .
>
> (Isa. 65:11, Moffatt.)

The rabbis of the Second Temple were bitterly opposed to these imported fashions. With disdain they speak "of those that play at dice, who calculate with their left hand, and press with their right, and rob and wrong one another." [3] Gamblers were excluded from the office of magistrate and from the Jewish courts. Their testimony was not trusted. Money gained by gambling was looked upon as money acquired by theft, except a Jew win it from a Gentile.[4] Money lost in gambling, since stolen, could not be regained in the courts.

Whether it be on the upward or downward position of musselfish in Siam, on coconut husking in the Philippines, or on "heads" or "tails" in early Rome, gambling is surely as old and almost as widespread as man. However, anthropologist A. L. Kroeber has dis-

[2] Virgil Peterson, *Gambling: Should It Be Legalized?* (Springfield, Ill.: Charles C. Thomas, Publisher, 1951), pp. 48 ff.
[3] *The Jewish Encyclopedia,* "Gambling," V, 563.
[4] Ludovici, *op. cit.,* p. 24.

covered a few primitive cultures where gambling is nonexistent.[5] This should indicate that gambling is an acquired habit associated with certain cultural traits. It is not an instinctive urge like eating or mating.

THE CHRISTIAN ERA

1. *The early period.* The Christian Church inherited from Judaism a deep concern for the purity of life, a strict stewardship of possessions, and hence a disdain for gambling.

The early Church Fathers and the Councils clearly condemned gambling among all Christians. Canon law forbade games of chance from very earliest times. Two of the oldest church laws threatened excommunication of clergy and laity alike for such participation. The Council of Elvira (*ca.* 306 A.D.) decreed that one of the faithful who had been guilty of gambling might be, on amendment, restored to communion after a penalty of one year. Clement of Alexandria, Tertullian, and others spoke strongly against gaming. "If you say that you are a Christian when you are a dice-player," said Tertullian, "you say you are what you are not, because you are a partner with the world." [6]

Such ideals and admonitions did not keep the Christians free from the immoral influences of the Greek and Roman culture that surrounded them. Indeed, gambling devices have been found in some early Christian tombs.

2. *Medieval morals.* When the world moved into the Church after Constantine, it was increasingly difficult to maintain the high standards of moral purity for the Christian life. Medieval man was a coarse and brutal animal. Gambling was prominent among his

---

[5] *Anthropology* (New York: Harcourt, Brace and World, Inc., 1948), pp. 552-53.
[6] *Encyclopedia of Religion and Ethics,* VII, 164.

vices. The Church repeatedly raised objections. Laws were passed, but little was done to stamp out the widespread practice. A twelfth-century writer characterizes Constantinople, the head of the Eastern church, as surpassing all other cities in wealth and vice.[7] Gambling halls and saloons were everywhere. "French laws of 1256 and 1291 forbade making, or playing with, dice, but gambling with dice was widespread nonetheless, and moralists told of fortunes and souls lost in the game." [8]

Gambling became popular with the clergy as well. Cardinal Raffaello Piario won 14,000 ducats in two games with the son of Pope Innocent VIII. This occurred even though the Fourth Lateran Council in 1215 forbade clerics to play or be present at games of chance. The renaissance popes were not noted for their piety nor their moral principles. Leo X was as addicted to card playing for stakes as many of his subjects were in the late fifteenth century.[9]

The medieval period is marked by the repeated attempts of church and state to restrict the gambling propensities of a rather superficial Christendom. "In Venice gambling ruined so many noble families that the Council of Ten twice forbade the sale of cards or dice, and called upon servants to report their masters violating these ordinances." Laws established by Savonarola in Florence in 1495 required from borrowers a pledge that they would not gamble at least until the loan had been repaid.[10] The Council of Trent which sought to bring reform to the Roman Catholic Church after the Protestant Reformation gathered and codified the ancient laws against gambling. The clergy were to abstain from unlawful games. No restrictions were addressed to the laity. From

[7] Will Durant, *The Age of Faith* (*The Story of Civilization* [New York: Simon and Schuster, Inc., 1950]), IV, 433.

[8] *Ibid.*, IV, 838.

[9] Durant, *The Renaissance, ibid.*, V, 595.

[10] *Ibid.*

this point to the present Roman Catholic thought has considerably moderated on the subject.

3. *Protestant positions.* The Geneva of John Calvin's day was as vicious in its gambling, prostitution, and drunkenness as any medieval town. All this Calvin set himself to sweep away. In his ordinances for the supervision of country churches, he wrote: "No one is to play at games that are dissolute, or at games played for gold or silver or at excessive expense, on pain of five sous and loss of the sum staked." [11] Immoderate gambling appears to be his point of attack.

Martin Luther recalled the Roman Church's restrictions against gambling in his youth. "When I was a boy all games were forbidden, so that cardmakers, pipers, and actors were not admitted to the sacraments; and those who had played games or been present at shows or plays, made it a matter of confession." (The puritanical strain of some medieval Catholicism is often overlooked.) In a treatise on usury Luther tackled the problem of gambling himself. "Money won by gambling . . . is not won without self-seeking and love of self, and not without sin." [12]

4. *Modern developments.* In modern English history the common law places no restrictions on gambling. Gambling is strictly a "creature of statue"; that is, the laws against gambling were introduced by king or parliament. Generally they came, not from a basic moral objection, but because gambling interferred with the militarily strategic sport of archery, and because the gambling dens frequently made themselves a public nuisance and financial detriment to the community.

During the reign of Queen Elizabeth I every attempt was made

[11] *Library of Christian Classics,* XXII, *Calvin: Theological Treatises* (Philadelphia: The Westminster Press, 1954), p. 82.

[12] *Works of Martin Luther* (Philadelphia: The Muhlenberg Press, 1931), IV, 58.

by the government to promote lotteries. They generally failed because of public reluctance. Even the Virginia Colony lottery of 1612 failed after various artificial attempts were made to whip up popular enthusiasm.

During the Puritan Commonwealth the heavy hand of legal control was laid upon the gambling habits of the English, and a cleanup was desirable. With the restoration of the monarchy under Charles II, however, the dike burst and England was inundated with a flood of moral anarchy. The gambling fever swept across seventeenth-century Europe with monstrous excess. By the following century even the papacy was sponsoring multiple lotteries every Saturday night with all the pious trimmings of a priestly blessing. The fact still remained that the great majority were losers for the causes of the church.

5. *Wesley on wagering.* England was an open sore of gin and gambling in the eighteenth century. John Wesley responded to both in his declaration of Christian purity for life. It should be acknowledged, however, that Wesley occasionally used lots to determine the Lord's will in a debated situation. This practice he received from the Moravians. Against criticism he insisted the lot was not used except in cases of continued disagreement after long prayer and debate. Even then, he insisted, the matter was not settled by chance, for "the whole disposal thereof is of the Lord." [13] A practice not unrelated to this was Wesley's way of dipping into the Bible at random to find God's direction in the first verse chanced upon. Again Wesley would insist the choice was directed by God.

As in the practice of ancient Israel, John Wesley radically separated divination from gambling, though we may admit one has derived from the other. Discussing the deceit and fraud general in

[13] *The Works of John Wesley* (Grand Rapids, Mich.: Zondervan Publishing House), VIII, 451.

English commerce, he deplored not only the "sharpers and game-sters (those public nuisances, those scandals to the English nation,)" but also the so-called respectable folk who applaud every such injustice in the greed for gain.[14] Those who played at cards were not allowed to continue in the Methodist Societies.[15]

THE GAMBLIN'EST NATION OF 'EM ALL

The Europeans who settled the new world brought their gambling games with them. New England Puritans censured gambling not so much on moral grounds as upon its rivalry of God's powers. According to Cotton Mather, "lots, being mentioned in the sacred oracles of Scripture as used only in weighty cases and as an acknowledgement of God sitting in judgement . . . cannot be made the tools and parts of our common sports, without, at least, such an appearance of evil as is forbidden in the word of God." [16] Lots, cards, and dice were banned in Massachusetts and Connecticut in the 1670's.

The Southern colonies witnessed gambling on every conceivable game, principally on the most brutal imports from England—bear-baiting, gander pulling, and cockfighting.

The beginning of the Methodist Church in America is related to Barbara Heck's repudiation of cardplaying. In 1765 she broke up a card game in New York and appealed to Philip Embury, a local Methodist preacher lately arrived from Ireland, "to preach to us or we shall all go to hell."

In several of the colonies lotteries were legal and widespread in the early 1700's. Columbia, Harvard, Yale, Dartmouth, and Williams colleges were financed in part in this way. Christ Church,

[14] *Ibid.*, p. 164.
[15] *The Letters of John Wesley* (London: The Epworth Press, 1931), VIII, 12.
[16] Quoted in Chafetz, *op. cit.*, p. 14.

Protestant Episcopal, in Philadelphia raised a steeple in 1753 through funds acquired by a lottery. Benjamin Franklin, John Hancock, and George Washington can be quoted in their support of public lotteries for public causes. Even a proposed national lottery had the support of Thomas Jefferson. As a means of raising public monies the lottery seemed an only out in face of the limited credit and the rejection of taxes by a poor people.

By the 1830's, however, every state in the Union had repudiated the lottery for public finance. Many had passed stringent laws against all forms of gambling. This was not because of the pressure of religious groups. Rather, the fraud, the economic ills, the relatively small amounts derived for worthy causes, led business leaders and politicians to repudiate legalized gambling. It had become apparent over a period of time that the lottery business defied all efforts at control. The racketeers won; the people lost. William Christie MacLeod observed:

the great mass of worthy citizens of New York and Massachusetts and Pennsylvania a century ago was opposed to public lotteries, not on abstract ethical grounds, but on the ground that they had become a serious social evil. . . . The campaigners against lotteries were primarily businessmen and professional men who saw around them everywhere the growing menace of the public lottery of the day.[17]

Newspapers in New York, Baltimore, Philadelphia, and Boston reported the gambling corruption and called upon citizens to rise up and drive the gamblers out. In some cases rioting citizens did just this.

Forced out of the Eastern cities, wide-open gambling went West

[17] "The Truth About Lotteries in American History," *The South Atlantic Quarterly* (April, 1936), pp. 201-11.

with the frontier. On the riverboats of the Midlands, in the frontier saloons of the cattle country, in the mining camps of the far West prosperity was measured by the volume of the "sucker trade." The Methodist missionary, and later Bishop, William Taylor wrote from San Francisco in 1850 of ministers who "swear and curse, of deacons seen at the gambling tables and church members watching their successes at roulette, faro or monte bank. And I have heard that the professed gamblers say, that money is so plenty and easy to be made and consequently betting is so high that it is necessary for them to cheat more than usual, to hold their own." [18]

New Orleans was the queen city of gamedom. Gambling flourished without prohibition there until 1811, when the legislature passed a bill restricting gambling. The lack of adequate law enforcement enabled the gambling fraternity to proceed with business as usual.

During the carpetbagger era one of the most sinister legalized gambling operations in the history of the country was stampeded into being. Organizers paid 50,000 dollars in bribes to secure legislative approval for the Louisiana Lottery Company in 1869. Continued graft paid to the state government reduced the income of the company over the first few years, but with clever promotion the company grew in opulence and political influence. For twenty years it controlled the state of Louisiana. The company's political machine tried to influence the disputed presidential election of 1876. It bought politicians and newspapers and diversified its investments. One third of the income of the New Orleans post office was due to the lottery mail. With an income of 30,000,000 dollars a year only a pittance was turned over to the charitable causes fronting for it.

By 1890 growing opposition from state and federal leaders

[18] Quoted in Chafetz, *op. cit.*, p. 119.

threatened the Louisiana gambling machine. President Benjamin Harrison, in a special message to Congress on July 30, 1890, called for federal laws which would curtail the "corrupting touch" of the Louisiana Lottery throughout the United States. Congress enacted a law prohibiting the use of the United States mails for the transmission of lottery tickets. In Louisiana, with the debauchery of twenty-five years in the minds of the voters, an anti-gambling slate of state officers was elected. The lottery company was dispatched in 1894 and operated unsuccessfully in Honduras for a few years.

Throughout the nineteenth century American Protestant churches condemned gambling. All too frequently the religious man was defined in a negative way as one who doesn't drink, smoke, fight, swear, gamble, dance, or go to the theater. In 1890 the Methodist Episcopal Church, South, entered the public forum against the Louisiana Lottery Company. "The *New Orleans Advocate* urged the circulation of petitions against it, carried in its pages a form of memorial to be sent to the state legislature, and urged its subscribers not to vote for any candidate who was under the influence of the scheme's promoters." [19]

So, after considerable experimentation with legalized gambling, especially the lottery, most American states have legally prohibited various forms of gambling. Nevada is a notorious exception. Prohibitions against gambling are written into the constitutions of many states.

TWENTIETH-CENTURY DEVELOPMENTS

The nineteenth and twentieth centuries have seen waves of popularity for horse-race gambling. Alternately, waves of righteous public indignation have rejected the race track and its attendant

---

[19] Richard M. Cameron, *Methodism and Society in Historical Perspective* (Nashville: Abingdon Press, 1961), p. 220.

corruption. Early in the twentieth century the neighborhood pool hall, equipped with Western Union hookup for direct track results, was frequently the local bookmaker. Regular payoffs for policemen and politicians allowed the illegal bookmaker to push his trade unmolested. Such corruption, and the violent competition of the underworld for the control of lucrative gambling areas, brought about a reform movement across the country against race gambling. Early in the twentieth century betting on the horses became illegal in many states. After January 1, 1911, gambling was permitted at tracks in only six states—Maryland, Oklahoma, Montana, Kentucky, Virginia, and Utah.[20]

During the depression of the thirties and during World War II gambling and graft took another increase in the urban areas. Political corruption, gambling, and crime are the unholy trinity exposed in Chicago, Kansas City, New Orleans, Cincinnati, and Buffalo. Through Tom Pendergast gamblers controlled the Kansas City police department and state elections. Men like Frank Costello, Lucky Luciano, and Charles Binaggio attended the national political conventions in style. Racketeering was organized on big-business lines, and comity agreements parceled out the gambling areas among the mobs. During the depression gambling continued to make the poor poorer for the sake of the enterprising operators. Bank nights, chain letters, and pyramid clubs were the craze.

A Gallup Poll in 1938 reported that 29 per cent of the adult American populace had gambled the previous year. The gambling population climbed during the war years. The American Institute of Public Opinion discovered the percentage of adult Americans gambling had climbed to 45 per cent in 1945, not including men in the armed forces. In 1950 55 per cent cheerfully admitted gam-

[20] Chafetz, op. cit., p. 298.

bling, in many cases illegally. The categories were: Church lotteries, 37 per cent; elections and athletic events, 23 per cent; bingo, 21 per cent; cards or dice for money, 19 per cent; punchboards, 18 per cent; slot machines, 15 per cent; races and sweepstakes, 13 per cent; numbers, 5 per cent. Since many did more than one of the above the total adds to more than 55 per cent. And of all these only one in seven who gambled admitted coming out ahead.[21] Sucker bait to be sure!

1. *Nevada—a fever.* In the midst of an Idaho gubernatorial race in which the democratic candidate was running on a ticket in support of legalized gambling, former President Truman said: "If you want to be like Nevada, that's your business. Nevada is the only black spot on the United States continent. So go ahead and do what you damn well please. . . . Legalized gambling is the worst thing in the world. I don't believe in it. Too many people have jumped out of windows because of Nevada. It is a fever." [22] It was 1931 when Nevada made gambling legal—practically everything except lotteries. The plan of state supervision worked pretty well during the quiet thirties. With the war boom of the forties Nevada gambling became big business and the center of organized crime in the United States. Tightened state control in 1945 endeavored to wrest power from underworld operators, but criminals managed to rig respectable fronts in the ownership of swank gambling casinos in Las Vegas, Reno, and Lake Tahoe. Disclosures of the fifties showed that Frank Costello and other hoods had controlling stock in several of the operations. In December, 1963, eleven nationally known gangsters —some associated with the gangland crime convention at Apalachin, New York, in 1957—were under indictment and suspicion

[21] Gallup, "More Than Half of Us Gamble," *Gambling in America,* pp. 25 ff.
[22] *New York Times* (September 30, 1962).

of holding hidden ownerships in the gambling establishments of Nevada.

The presence of criminal elements and powerful syndicates in the background of Nevada gambling is not due to official laxity, says Virgil Peterson, director of the Chicago Crime Commission. "The fault lies with the business itself. It has always attracted the underworld and past experience clearly reflects that the racketeering and criminal element will always be prominently identified with the gambling business." [23]

The amount of revenue from gambling received by the large spaced, sparsely populated state of Nevada is variously reported. According to Ludovici one source claims an income of 18,000,000 dollars a year from gambling for the state or about one half of the state's expenses. Another credits gambling revenues as only 6½ per cent of the total state income. The Nevada Gaming Commission claims for 1962 a state income of 11,263,463 dollars or 20.2 per cent of all revenue to be from the gambling tables.[24] The boomtown, Las Vegas, is reported to need five sixths more revenue for its municipal government than that provided by gambling taxation. Only one of the largest Nevada casino operators nets 40,000,000 dollars a year over against the annual cost of 36,000,000 dollars to operate the state of Nevada.

President Truman's statement arises out of the obvious social blight from gambling in the state of Nevada. Reno has the highest crime rate of any city in the United States in proportion to its population. Its suicides are twice the American average. It ranks in murders with cities four times its size. Four times as many police-

---

[23] *Gambling: Should It Be Legalized?* op. cit., p. 91.
[24] Ludovici, *op. cit.*, p. 202; *Legalized Gambling in Nevada* (Carson City: Nevada Gaming Commission, 1962), p. 24.

men are needed than the American average for a comparable population. Welfare and other state costs are abnormal.[25]

These feverish Nevada cities of bright neon lights, fast entertainment, call girls, and constant gambling are never closed. Customers are hauled in by plane and bus from as far away as Chicago. The middle-class patron is now being invited by all kinds of conscience-easing "hidden persuaders." Gambling has been developed specifically in the center of the Lake Tahoe summer and winter sports area so as to give the troubled conscience of middle-class Americans an out. Gambling losses can all be written off as a vacation for the family.[26] Indeed, many of the American Express tours of the United States for foreign visitors include these Nevada hotspots as important stops in their roundup of genuine Americana.

2. *Recent developments.* In 1962 the 575-member National College Athletic Association sought Congressional action to make sports bribery a federal offense. The action by the colleges arises out of a decade of basketball, football, and baseball bribery scandals. Amateur players especially have been susceptible to point shaving for the payoff of the bookmakers.

The Kennedy administration stepped up the federal warfare against organized crime and gambling. New legislation has curtailed the interstate transmission of gambling paraphernalia and information—parlay cards, race wire services, and slot machines—except to states where they are legal. This has hurt organized illegal gambling. The Justice Department has increased its prosecution of federal gambling violations. Convictions are up considerably.

Recent legalization of bingo for charitable causes in the state of New York has been proved riddled with corruption and excessive

[25] Ludovici, *op. cit.,* p. 203.
[26] *Ibid.,* pp. 196 ff.

profit for the operators in spite of state supervision. Opposed by Protestant and Jewish leaders, the bill has been defended principally by veterans' organizations and the Roman Catholic Church.

The year 1963 saw an increased tempo in the extension of legalized gambling. Governor John King of New Hampshire signed into law a sweepstakes lottery bill predicted to reap 4,000,000 dollars annually beginning in 1964 for state educational institutions. Maine, California, and Vermont are interested in the New Hampshire experiment.[27] Pennsylvania and Vermont legalized pari-mutuel betting for the first time in the states' history. Eleven states extended the allowable season for racing, and several upped the state's cut of the race gambler's dollar. Mayor Robert Wagner of New York City pressed for the legalization and taxation of off-track betting for an estimated 100,000,000 dollars in revenue. Illinois considered a bill to permit year-round racing. The state of Maryland, in spite of its increase of racing days, enacted legislation to provide for a gradual elimination of slot machines in four southern Maryland counties.

In Texas business leaders contributed 167,000 dollars to promote racing. San Antonio legislator Virgil Berry told a ministerial association that it need not fear that racing would lure prostitutes. "We already got plenty of prostitutes to meet the demands," he said. A racing bill was favorably reported out of an Iowa legislative subcommittee. A pari-mutuel horse-racing bill was introduced each session in the Missouri state legislature by so-called "horse-breeding" interests. In Idaho, where at least five previous legislatures passed a pari-mutuel law only to see governors veto it, the 1963 legislature overrode Governor Robert Smylie's veto.[28] The state of Washington

[27] *Time* (April 5, 1963), p. 29.
[28] *Ibid.*

47

passed a new bill legalizing pinball machines and other forms of gambling.[29]

Other states have evidenced interest in the revenue-from-gambling approach without direct taxes on the public. At the same time we hear the echoes of the Kefauver Crime Commission hearings of a decade ago. Today we note the increased prosecution of crime-related gambling by the United States Justice Department. Gangland killings between underworld gambling competitors continue. These should keep the American people aware of the vicious and criminal nature of organized gambling—even when legalized.

CONCLUSION

Those advocating legalized gambling like to dismiss their opponents with the charge of puritanism.[30] Our historical survey has shown that opposition to gambling is not primarily puritan in origin. "Mass gambling has *always* resulted in great social and economic ills: and almost every civilized nation in the world has from time to time found it necessary to resort to repressive legislation in an effort to protect its citizens." [31] The pattern of the past shows "legalization schemes have in turn increased mass gambling to the extent that the nation has found it necessary to enact prohibitory laws." This has been true in Great Britain, in the case of the early American lotteries, and in latter days with the slot machines in Florida, Idaho, and Maryland.

Assistant United States Attorney General Herbert Miller of the Justice Departments' criminal division replied for Attorney General

[29] *New York Times* (May 12, 1963), p. 66.

[30] See Governor John King's self-righteous defense of the New Hampshire sweepstakes bill which he signed into law in April of 1963 over the protest of Protestant and Jewish leaders, *This Week Magazine* (July 14, 1963).

[31] Virgil Peterson, "A History of Legalized Gambling," *The Annals of the American Academy of Political and Social Science.*

Robert Kennedy to a request for an opinion on the New Hampshire sweepstake. He said, in part:

The history of lotteries in this country indicates that each time a state used them, as a source of revenue, a large share of the take went to the promoters of the lottery in spite of the control enacted along with the lottery legislation.

. . . Corruption of officials charged with the administration of the lottery seems to have taken place as a matter of course. . . . [The lottery] is attractive principally to the ignorant and people who can least afford to gamble.[32]

[32] *The Christian Century* (May 22, 1963), p. 685.

3

THE SOCIAL CONSEQUENCES

"Gambling is the biggest single cause of such crimes as embezzlement; it also is a cause of broken marriages, neglected children, poverty and sometimes suicide." So wrote Ernest Havemann for the readers of *Life* magazine.[1] Havemann is himself an inveterate player of the ponies. Havemann's honest admission of the social consequences of gambling deserves our attention. Besides all the fun and the froth there is an inevitable social sewage left in the wake of the frolic.

INCREASED CRIME

1. *Embezzlements and theft.* In Los Angeles a city employee embezzled more than 50,000 dollars over a period of years in municipal

[1] June 19, 1950, p. 109

funds. Why? To pay for his bets on the horses. After visiting him in San Quentin, his minister reported him to be "a bewildered, broken man."

A New York City longshoreman played regularly in a daily dice game on the docks. He lost heavily and borrowed from loan sharks. At their suggestion he started thieving items from the docks to pay the sharks. Finally a whole group of workingmen were arrested for stealing on the docks. He was one of them.

Virgil Peterson names gambling and extravagant living as the two major causes of embezzlement by executives. The story of respectable folk in responsible positions who embezzle funds and embroider the ledgers to cover their gambling losses is an old one. Among the lower economic groups petty theft frequently serves the same purposes. A study of embezzlements made by the United States Fidelity and Guaranty Company of Baltimore shows that of the 4,000,000 dollars embezzled in 1947, from 30 to 75 per cent of this sum was attributed to gambling.[2]

The exceptionally high crime rate in the state of Nevada is to be explained by this social consequence of wide-open gambling. A recent report from the Federal Bureau of Investigation shows that the gambling states have a generally higher crime rate. The national rate is 1,052.8 offenses per 100,000 population; for non-gambling states, 906.7; for gambling states, 1,756.3. Nevada leads the percentages with a report of 1,993.1, and as a city Reno tops them all with 3,061.1 offenses per 100,000 population. Las Vegas is the second highest city in the United States with a percentage of 2,760.8.[3]

2. *Gambling and organized crime.* "Gambling," says Virgil W.

---

[2] David D. Allen, *The Nature of Gambling* (New York: Coward-McCann, Inc., 1952), p. 78.
[3] FBI Uniform Crime Report for 1963.

Peterson, "is the backbone of crime in America, an integral part of corrupt politics and corrupt police." Many people assume that their two-dollar bet is a very personal matter—a transgression quite innocent of the law. How could the local newsman, the pool-hall operator, or that nice guy who collects on the football pools at the factory be dangerous?

Attorney General Robert F. Kennedy answered this question for a House subcommittee considering legislation to curb organized crime and racketeering in May, 1961. "Many persons think of the corner handbook operator or the neighborhood merchant, who sells a numbers ticket to him, as the person to whom we refer when we talk of the gambling racketeer." This is only the top of the gambling iceberg, however. To see the full danger and size of the problem, as with the iceberg, we must go below the surface.

The handbook operator is the float on the surface. He profits from the persons placing bets with him because he has an edge on their bets. He pays track odds but usually not in excess of 20 to 1. The odds at the track are calculated after deducting the 15 per cent to 18 per cent of the total betting pool. This goes for taxes and other expenses. The illegal bookmaker pockets this "cream off the top" which would otherwise go to the state and the track.

He is not a man of unlimited resources, however. He must balance his books. He can lose no more on the winner than has been bet on the other horses in a race, after his percentage has been deducted. He cannot control the choices of his customers. Frequently he will find that the horse that is their favorite is not the track favorite. His "action," as he calls it, may not reflect the action of the track. He must therefore reinsure himself on the race. This will be done in much the same way as a casualty insurance company reinsures a risk too great for it to assume alone. To do this the bookmaker uses the "layoff" man, who, for a commission, accepts the excess wager.

The local layoff bettor also has limited funds, and when his layoff bets are out of balance he calls the large layoff bettors who can spread the larger risk. This is where the nationwide syndicate or combine of gamblers comes in. The members of this combine are in close touch with each other all the time. They distribute the bets among themselves so that an overall balance is reached on any horse race or ball game.

With a balanced book at the local handbook, layoff, or syndicate level the edge is divided and no one loses except the man who placed the original bet. Attorney General Kennedy indicated the volume of business he was speaking of—"one of the largest operators in the combine does a layoff business of $18 million a year. His net profit is $720,000 a year. This is a 4 per cent return on volume, with relatively no risk, as a result of the balancing of his books on each event." [4] Fred Cook estimates there are 50,000 master bookies and some 400,000 small fry operating in the United States in the above manner. This means a small army of organized criminals operating in major communities throughout the nation.

The tremendous profits from this kind of enterprise are believed to be the treasure chest of the underworld in this country and abroad. Attorney General Kennedy expressed this quite clearly in his *Atlantic* article:

No one knows exactly how much money is involved in gambling in the United States. What we do know is that the American people are spending more on gambling than on medical care or education; that, in so doing, they are putting up the money for the corruption of public

---

[4] "The Baleful Influence of Gambling," *The Atlantic Monthly* (April, 1962), p. 77.

officials and the vicious activities of the dope peddlers, loan sharks, boot-
leggers, white-slave traders, and slick confidence men.

Investigation this past year by the FBI, Internal Revenue Service, the
Narcotics Bureau, the Post Office Department, and all other federal
investigative units has disclosed without any shadow of a doubt that
corruption and racketeering, financed largely by gambling, are weaken-
ing the vitality and strength of this nation.[5]

The cash that Mr. and Mrs. America lose on gambling may help
to provide the down payment on a brothel or to start a narcotics
salesman on a new route. Professional gamblers operate in every
community by intimidation, the politician-policeman pay-off, open
violence, and murder. In spite of all the suave insinuations of Mr.
Lucky on television, the business of gambling is not clean, not
glamorous, not gentle. "Scratch a gambler," said Edward Silver,
District Attorney in Brooklyn, "and you find a murderer."

In 1958 a Brooklyn grand jury made an extensive special study
of gambling that would corroborate Silver's statement. The grand
jury found indisputable links between illegal gambling and "the
most obnoxious criminal enterprises known to man." They also
pointed to the gambling connections of several gangland killings
in Brooklyn over the past few years. One case involved seven narcotics dealers, six of whom were engaged in bookmaking and policy,
which they used as the source of funds for their deadly trade in
dope. The attempted assassination of Frank Costello, czar of New
York crime, May 2, 1957, revealed his close associations with the so-
called clean, legal gambling of Nevada. Notes from his pockets
showed an accounting on his investment in the Las Vegas Tropi-
cana casino-hotel through a dummy corporation. Just ten years
before Buggsy Siegel, the western crime organizer for New York

[5] *Ibid.,* p. 76.

and Chicago syndicates, failed to escape the gangland assassin's bullets. Siegel financed and operated the Flamingo in Las Vegas.

In 1955 the Nevada Gaming Control Board was reorganized and charged to "get tough" with the hoods. Even so they could not weed out Costello. Now just recently, the Justice and Internal Revenue Departments of the federal government have greatly increased their surveillance of Nevada's so-called clean gambling. Bob Whearley of the *Denver Post* reports they believe the big time gambler-hoodlums have moved in on the big money again. In his ten article series on "The Truth About Las Vegas" he says the federal men believe as much as 25 per cent of the casino winnings may come off the top to be deposited in Swiss or Panamanian banks. Later these funds will be plowed back into the rackets—large scale narcotics and prostitution, among others. There is some indication that Raymond J. Abbaticchio was not reappointed Chairman of Nevada's Gaming Control Board in 1961 because he was too tough on the gangsters in the Las Vegas casinos.

So the story could be continued about the corruption of entire communities by the criminal elements which operate through legal and illegal gambling—Beaumont, Texas; Phoenix City, Alabama; Newport, Kentucky; not to speak of "crime's fifty-first state, New York City."

POLITICAL POLLUTION

The amounts of money involved in the gambling industry "are so tremendous that the expenditure of large sums of money for the corruption of enforcement officials, and officials at even higher levels, can and is absorbed as an expense of doing business." So reported the Kefauver Crime Commission a decade ago. Recent attempts were made to bribe a legislator to "take a walk or vote 'no' " on an anti-slots bill. Such brazen bribery attempts in the halls of the Maryland statehouse helped to focus on the corruption involved and pass the prohibitory legislation.

The stranglehold of legal or illegal gambling upon state politics and law enforcement has already been told in the case of the Louisiana Lottery Company. What is not so clear is the duplication of such government corruption all over the nation. One of our most astute political analysts, Andrew D. White, has made the widely quoted observation: "With very few exceptions the city governments of the United States are the worst in Christendom—the most expensive, the most inefficient and the most corrupt. And to this gambling has largely contributed." [6]

Reports from independent crime commissions in Chicago, New Orleans, Boston, and New York point to the widespread corruption of law enforcement officers in high and low places. Gambling and vice have operated wide open with the obvious knowledge of the police—even after independent notice of such operations. One of the most successful exposures of police and political corruption was made by "CBS Reports" in a film documentary entitled "Biography of a Bookie Joint." Hidden cameras had recorded the activities of a Boston bookmaker operating behind a keymaker's shop front. The camera recorded a steady stream of gambling patrons in undoubtedly the busiest keyshop in the nation. Included were several members of the Boston police department in uniform. Periodically the operators would destroy records in an ash can on the street in front of the shop. The shop was openly known to everyone, including the federal agency which raided it. Yet it had enjoyed its lucrative illegality undisturbed by the city police except for their patronage. The television camera showed the whole nation the close relationship between gambling and graft—the paid silence of the crooked cop. After this exposure there were resignations and prose-

[6] Lodovici, *op. cit.*, p. 185.

cutions in Massachusetts law-enforcement agencies. Charges and counter charges echoed from the precinct level to top political offices in the statehouse. The Massachusetts Crime Commission commented:

It seems to have been a universal finding by crime survey commissions that organized illegal gambling could not exist within a community without the knowledge and the protection of the local police. For all practical purposes that is a fair statement. . . . The existence of an illegal gambling operation is as apparent as any other type of retail business. The place to which customers come, such as a horse room, the location of a card or dice game or of pinball machines, is more than apparent; it is obvious. The idea that games float to hide from police is more fiction than fact. Gaming operators have told the commission that they move to avoid complaint, not arrest. . . .

Protection is a state that occurs as frequently by the demand of the police as by the offer of the racketeer. . . . The universal complaint among gaming operators is that the demands have been becoming increasingly exorbitant. Some have told the Commission that the price of protection has reached the stage where illegal gambling is *police business instead of bookie business.* . . .[7]

If a policeman wants to be honest he may be given the graveyard patrol. He is not likely to report much "action" there—or to get a promotion. Elected officials who outrank him may make the honest road a most difficult one. Politicians are most subject to obligation and conflict of interest by accepting campaign contributions and workers from the gambling syndicates. David Hume, who was a candidate for governor in the 1962 Democratic primary in Maryland revealed the extent of the gambling pressure on political candidates there. He told a House of Delegates committee that "all politicians

[7] Quoted in Cook, *op. cit.*, p. 259.

must take contributions from them [the slot machine operators] to survive." [8]

Politicians and policemen bribed to go soft on gambling are in no position to refuse the underworld in its extension of vice throughout a community. It is obvious, in America at least, that the huge gambling industry has been thoroughly claimed by criminal syndicates and underworld associations. The easy profits from gambling flow into the coffers of the rackets. Legal and illegal gambling survive through intimidation and graft. Such political pollution is the inevitable consequence of a business which suckers easy billions out of the weaknesses of a people.

ECONOMIC WASTE

This brings us to the unusual economic nature of the gambling industry itself. In many respects the nation's largest business, gambling, serves no community need. Of course, the systematic plundering of the public purse might be termed recreation; but if recreation, it comes at a completely unjustifiable cost. The artificial risks of gambling do not serve to house, feed, or finance in the manner of the rest of the business community. As we have seen, most of the profits from gambling are used to exploit the further weaknesses of the people. Very little of the consumer's dollar returns to the marketplace to strengthen the community economy. Gambling produces no goods or wealth for exchange. In the case of legal gambling only a small portion of the public investment is used by the state for public services. The higher costs of gambling-related public protection and welfare service may more than offset income. Gambling siphons off the salaries, savings, and investments of a community for a business enterprise that serves no human need. Those who benefit from this redistribution of wealth already pro-

[8] *Washington Post* (March 1, 1963).

duced are generally among the most antisocial elements of a country.

There are many indications of the parasitic nature of gambling upon the business community. History shows this to be one reason for recurrent anti-gambling legislation. Reporting on the effects of dog racing upon Portland and the state of Oregon, Senator Richard L. Neuberger wrote in September, 1951:

When the gambling is going full blast, so are the collection agencies. People behind on their doctor's or grocery bills often show up in the pari-mutuel lines. Many merchants detect an immediate slump in payments when the greyhounds start running. A nightly "handle" of nearly $250,-000 in a non-resort community can only be taken out of the goods and services produced by residents. The movie business falls apart when the track is strong. The baseball park is virtually empty.[9]

Always more difficult to eliminate than to acquire, wide-open state-approved gambling in Florida was reduced with beneficial effects to the state's economy. Some argued that gambling was purely entertainment and tourists ought to be able to gamble if they wanted to. Governor Leroy Collins didn't believe this. He pointed to the tourist shakedown by sharpies in Florida and the moral influence of racketeering upon the citizenry. Slot machines were outlawed and anti-bookie statutes were strengthened. "The year after Daytona Beach closed down gambling," he said, "it did a much better tourist business than ever before, and it has improved consistently, attracting the kind of people who came as friends, not overnight fortune hunters."

From Maryland we hear a similar story. Gubernatorial candidate David Hume, a former trial attorney for the Department of Justice,

[9] "Oregon Goes to the Dogs," *Gambling in America,* edited by H. L. Marx, p. 106.

discussed the matter in the February 13, 1960, issue of *The Nation*. He calculated that legalization of slot machines has cost his home county, Charles County, Maryland, literally millions of dollars in normal, healthy growth. Hume recognized that slot-machine revenue did keep the tax rate down compared to nearby Montgomery County, but Montgomery County without the slots had developed into a fine residential suburb of the capital city. To the contrary Charles County with even finer natural resources had become wedded to the gambling honky-tonk. To get the benefit of approximately 400,000 dollars in gambling revenue the 30,000 residents of Charles County sacrificed more than 32,000,000 dollars in reduced land values.

A minimum of 100,000,000 dollars a year is drained out of Maryland by slots and illegal pay-off pinball machines. "This is an appalling drain on counties that are in need of economic development and a higher standard of living," says Richard W. Emory, head of Governor Tawe's study commission on gambling.

Gambling hurts industry. Governor Sawyer admits it is difficult to attract new industry to Nevada because of the presence of gambling, the consequent fear of absenteeism, and employee instability.[10] Illegal gambling infiltrates industry. Labor unions and employers have begun to cooperate against the inroads of professional gamblers in their factories and shops. Of concern is the hardship to working families, as well as the loss in work time and production. Back in 1948 *Business Week* made a two-month study of in-plant gambling in seven manufacturing centers. It was found generally that one out of every 250 employees of industry is also employed by a gambling syndicate as an in-plant agent. These agents made from 50 to 1,700 per cent of their legitimate wages in illegal income. One firm in New York City discovered an in-

[10] *Denver Post*, "The Truth about Las Vegas" (August 19, 1963).

crease of 20 to 25 per cent in production after a crackdown on gambling in the plant. The attempted assassination of Walter Reuther some years ago is undoubtedly related to his war on gambling within the auto plants of Detroit.

Gambling may appeal to 36,000,000 poverty-stricken Americans as a get-rich-quick way out of their misery. It may, at the other extreme, appeal to the insensitive rich as an easily afforded entertainment. "If you waste your money on something else, you sometimes at least have something in your hand to look at. It isn't gone without a trace." So comments John Sanford, editor of the *Reno Evening Gazette,* who believes Nevada's claim of gambling prosperity is an illusion.[11] It is an economic waste and a drain upon the public welfare.

A SOCIOLOGICAL COMMENT

In our society, with all its motivations toward economic success and status, gambling frequently represents the way up and out of the slums for the depressed classes. Work and some luck are believed to be the general ingredients in the American success story. For many hard work has not been the way up and out. A technological maze of economic ills often defies solution by one individual's earnest effort. For many, then, luck becomes the shortcut to success. Such motivations may affect the middle class as well as the poorer, depressed groups. The more one has the more he thinks he needs. This is especially true in an economy like ours, which operates on planned obsolescence and manipulated sales appetites.

Gambling seems to provide not only a way out for the economically depressed, but a way to endure as well. Many of our citizens are still hedged in by limited and uninspiring employment

[11] *New York Times* (May 19, 1963), p. 78.

—if they are employed—at low earning levels. Many lack the assurance of any possibility of genuine social and economic advancement. Among such groups, lacking vocational motivation and economic security, the pressures to gamble are fierce. Thus the "numbers" or "policy" game is called the poor man's lottery. The daily number purchased for a few cents is a way of life, a measure of hope, a cult for millions.

In his book *Man, Crime, and Society* Herbert Bloch suggested a triumvirate of reasons for the close association between gambling and crime in this country:

1. The outlawing of gambling, with the minor exception of private activities, some church-connected programs, and race-track settings, is one of the factors. (Bloch does acknowledge that the overall legalization of gambling would not solve the problem.)

2. A moral indifference toward gambling exists in a large segment of our society. This is especially true among the poorer groups. Industry and thrift are primarily middle-class virtues.

3. This moral attitude of consent is found among law-enforcement officers as well. Low salaries and the social background of the officers contribute to their indulgence in gambling and graft. The confusion of local laws and enforcement agencies in America also contributes to the on-again-off-again curtailment of gambling crime.[12]

CONCLUSION

"Gaming corrupts our dispositions and teaches us a habit of hostility against all mankind," said Thomas Jefferson in 1787. The social sewage of the gambling enterprise is obvious on all sides. Embezzlement and theft, high suicide rates, close association with

[12] See Bloch and Gilbert Geis (New York: Random House, Inc., 1962), p. 230.

syndicated crime, political and police pollution, economic waste—all are a part of the sorry spectacle. Gambling may increase our hostility toward all mankind, but it is also symptomatic of deeper distresses in our social structure—tedious and purposeless occupations, inequitable distribution of the nation's wealth, cheap and inconsistent law enforcement, the Horatio Alger myth of success by sweat in the face of insurmountable economic and social obstacles, the continued stress on personal initiative to the neglect of community responsibility. No solution for gambling corruption in a society may be found which ignores society's provocation of gambling.

4

GAMBLING MOTIVES

Why do people gamble? In face of unbeatable odds, manifest crookedness, and frequent social and religious disapproval why do a majority of American adults continue this prodigious waste of time and money?

During the Restoration period gambling went wild in England. From this time John Cotton's *Compleat Gamester* gives us a description of the gambler's fearful fascination. He said:

Gambling is an enchanting witchery, gotten between idleness and avarice: an itching disease that makes some scratch the head; while others, as if bitten by a tarantula, are laughing themselves to death. . . .

Gambling hath this ill property above all other vices, that it renders a man incapable of prosecuting any serious action, and makes him always unsatisfied with his own condition; he is either lifted up to the top of mad joy with success, or plunged to the bottom of despair by misfortune, always in extremes, always in a storm; this minute the gamester's countenance is so serene and calm that one would think nothing could disturb it, and the next minute, so stormy and tempestuous that it threatens destruction to itself and others; and as he is transported with joy when he wins, so losing, is he lost upon the billows of a high and swelling passion till he hath lost sight both of sense and reason.[1]

Similar descriptions of contemporary gamesters abound. *Look*'s senior editor, Gereon Zimmermann, began a feature article: "The gambler chases ecstasy, not money. His triumphant rapture is wondrous, fearful to behold." He quoted an Ivy Leaguer, "Going to the track is better than getting drunk. You forget everything." [2] Here is that swelling passion which loses sight of sense and reason that Cotton described in the seventeenth century.

Gambling is a sapling with many roots, a flourishing sapling symptomatic of deeper origins than would appear on the surface. We have already noted some sociological reasons for gambling. Following Cotton's clues, let us hunt for a few more of these roots—the "whys" of gambling.

"GOTTEN BETWEEN IDLENESS AND AVARICE"

The get-something-for-nothing attitude is abroad in the land. It disdains work and eschews craftsmanship, yet wants the benefits of the same—a high standard of living. The gambling mania, the give-away gimmicks in the marketplace, the sorry spectacle of easy money on TV quiz shows—all gotten without regard to services performed—tell us something about contemporary culture and its values.

[1] Quoted in Ludovici, *op. cit.*, p. 60.
[2] "Gambling," *Look* (March 12, 1963), p. 26.

The fast buck and the shoddy merchandise, the work slowdown and the moral wear-out, point to a crisis in the social order, to be sure.

Herbert Bloch speaks of a crisis when work is no longer considered a calling. The assembly line has taken the heart out of craftsmanship. Automation limits working days and increases leisure time. With these technological changes the predominant Puritan ethic of nineteenth-century Protestant America has either worn out or worn thin. The need for a new Christian understanding of work and leisure appropriate to our present technological setting is pressing.

The get-something-for-nothing attitude which motivates much gambling is not a strange new "social disease," however. Basically this malady is centuries old, listed among the seven deadly sins of medieval society. The Apostle Paul called it avarice and numbered it alongside sexual perversion and murder. We might term it greed. Long before Paul, Moses is reputed to have delivered the laws of God to his people, laws against covetousness and stealing.

Take away the greed for gain, the avarice for unearned riches, and gambling would lose its luster for many.

This attitude, "gotten between idleness and avarice," is psychologically damaging. It stifles personal initiative, integrity, and creativity. District Attorney Hogan of New York County has said, "I am unalterably opposed to legalized gambling. It would place a premium on shiftlessness and make a mockery of the virtues of hard work and thrift." What will happen to a society in which the majority of the people are convinced they can get something for nothing? Who will bake our bread, build our houses, and buy our produce? What will this attitude do to the individual's concern to develop his own God-given talents?

"AN ITCHING DISEASE . . .
LAUGHING THEMSELVES TO DEATH"

Some people gamble to satisfy deep-seated neurotic needs. In 1956 a minister's son, his wife, and his daughter disappeared one night from their middle-class home in an Eastern suburb. They left so abruptly that the second car was found in the garage with the key still in the ignition. The doors of the house were unlocked; the clock radio was on; an attached perculator of coffee bubbled in the kitchen. What had happened? Threatened and beaten by hoodlums, the young man and his family vanished to escape heavy gambling debts. Within a few months the family was separated. Later the husband wound up on skid row a victim, not of alcohol, but of compulsive gambling.

There are from 4 to 6,000,000 such compulsive gamblers in the United States.[3] For them gambling is an addiction. These are people who look to the gaming table as a solution, an escape, or a compensation for their personality problems. They may even seek punishment to salve a guilty conscience. George S. Stevenson, M.D., editor of *Mental Hygiene* and former medical consultant for the National Association for Mental Health, said,

Many people come to adult life suffering from a feeling of inadequacy about themselves and a feeling of uncertainty about life in general. Unable to meet the demands of life, they resort to roundabout measures for dealing with reality. They may develop neurotic symptoms. They may take to alcohol or narcotics. Or they may take to compulsive gambling. One turn of a card, one spin of the wheel, can make everything come out all right—they hope. But it seldom does. And even when gamblers win, the need to prove themselves, to quiet the self-doubt, is not assuaged. It keeps on asserting itself over and over again, plunging

[3] Bob Todd, "The Compulsive Gambler–II," *Washington Post* (April 12, 1963). *Cf.* Cole and Margolius, *op. cit.,* p. 15.

them compulsively into one disastrous adventure after another until reality asserts itself in the form of social or economic destruction.[4]

The Russian novelist Dostoevski was such a compulsive gambler. He pawned his wife's jewelry for money to lose at roulette. His novelette *The Gambler* is a hair-raising story of a wasted life. It is the story of a school tutor who became attracted to roulette by the great sums he believes may be won without the necessity of work. He became a man bound to the necessity of gambling because he was not fit to work. Friends were as reluctant to entrust him with money, even for his own miserable upkeep, as they would be reluctant to entrust an alcoholic with relief money for his family. He wanted to break clean of the habit: "Tomorrow, tomorrow," he said, "ah, but if only I could set things right tomorrow, and be born again, and rise again from the dead. Today is too late, but tomorrow." The book ends, as does the gambler's life we suspect, on the note of painful postponement.

Dostoevski's "gambler" illustrates all the six characteristics of the compulsive gambler:

1. He takes chances habitually.
2. The game precludes all his other interests—home, family, love, even life itself.
3. He is optimistic and will not learn from defeat.
4. He will not stop when winning.
5. He eventually risks too much.
6. A "pleasurable-painful tension" (thrill) is experienced during the game.[5]

---

[4] Introduction to "The Strangest Compulsion," *Good Housekeeping* (February, 1961), p. 80.

[5] Edmund Bergler, *The Psychology of Gambling* (New York: Hill & Wang, Inc., 1957), pp. 2-6.

Based on the study of sixty gambling addicts during thirty years of practice, psychiatrist Edmund Bergler believes the compulsive gambler is literally "laughing himself to death." He has a deep-seated unconscious need to lose, to be punished, to hurt himself. And what better way is there, than at continuous gambling?

Yet the compulsive gambler, said Bergler, believes he will win because he *wants* to win. His own omnipotent will declares it *shall* be so. Unconsciously he is still playing the infant who assumes that the world revolves around him, his own needs and demands. Rather than accept the attempts of his parents and educators to show him that reality does not center in his own omnipotence he has rebelled. He will show them; he will win. For this aggression against them he is driven into guilt. All this unconsciously motivates him at the gaming table. He *orders* the next card, the next throw of the dice, the next spin of the wheel to win. He will prove his omnipotence. At the same time he is overwhelmed by a sense of guilt. Although he occasionally wins, he continues to play because he really wants to lose. His guilt must be punished and expiated. Unconsciously he is a "glutton for punishment."

In a moment of irony at his own expense a humorous gambler confided in Dr. Bergler:

You know, I remind myself of the man who played the game of trying to guess which of his opponent's fists contained a silver dollar. In this game, if you choose correctly, you win a dollar; if not, you lose a dollar. In this instance, though, one man was cheating, and after the decision always managed to win by sleight of hand. An onlooker saw the swindle and asked the loser, "Don't you see that you are being cheated?" "Of course I see it," was the indignant answer, "but I must win back my money first." [6]

[6] *Ibid.*, pp. 238-39.

We laugh at this pathetic sucker, but this is a perfect picture of the compulsive gambler. He has lost a grip on reality and is naïvely optimistic that he will master the situation against all odds.

Robert M. Lindner continues the Freudian analysis of the gambler.[7] He agrees with Bergler's disclosure of the gambler's need to lose. He would add, however, the gambler's need to win at the same time. Unconsciously the gambler is troubled by a desire for the death of his father and incestuous designs upon his mother. Win or lose he is trapped either way. He is either omnipotent over his domineering father and guilty of incest, or his incestuous designs are indicated though he is guilty of patricide. The Freudian school of psychoanalysis relates gambling—as nearly everything else abnormal—to some form of sexual perversion.

Whatever else we may say about why the compulsive gambler gambles we must surely recognize that he is quite ill. He is an obsessional neurotic who desperately needs understanding and help. Gambling is a symptom of deeper personality distress. Yet gambling compounds the difficulty and adds to the distress. Here the gambler, like the neurotic who takes to alcohol or narcotics, seeks a solution which is not forthcoming. Social approval of drinking or gambling perpetuates his obsession by giving it a pseudo-rational respectability. Just now the public is becoming somewhat aware of the serious moral sickness of alcoholism and the alcoholic's need for understanding and treatment. Hardly anyone recognizes the equally serious nature of compulsive gambling, and few there be who care. Ministers, physicians, and psychiatrists have been unable to offer much aid.

Some who do care are Gambler's Anonymous. Like AA, GA began among addicts who wanted to stop and decided to try to

[7] "The Psychodynamics of Gambling," *The Annals of the American Academy of Political and Social Science* (May, 1950), pp. 93 ff.

help each other. The first chapter began in 1957 in California. Others, quite independent of any national organization, developed in the United States, Australia, and Ireland to a present number of fifty chapters. The only requirement for membership is a desire to stop gambling.

GA meetings are informal group therapy in which members admit, "I am a compulsive gambler," and then relate their experiences. Fellow members give criticism, encouragement, and support. There is no halfway stopping for the addict. He must give up gambling altogether and restructure his life around purposeful goals. Major problems for the ex-gambler are time and debt. Having spent much of his time gambling, he must now turn these hours to positive use. Also by the time he reaches Gambler's Anonymous he is probably head over heels in debt. When assured of his sincere reform the organization may make arrangements with his creditors and his employer to work out a second chance for financial recovery. Chances of recovery for the genuine GA participant are good. "Eight out of ten who join manage, in time, to stop gambling." These are odds on which even the compulsive gambler can afford to take a chance.

GA groups have developed wives' auxiliaries called GAMANON. If the family has remained together wives find themselves in need of group assistance also. They need to understand the peculiar nature of their husbands' addiction and to learn how they can help. The use of time and the balancing of the budget are problems for them also. Though we have spoken primarily of men as members of GA it is true that about one-third of the compulsive gamblers in this country are women.[8] Thus far none have

---

[8] "The Compulsive Gambler–III," *Washington Post* (April 19, 1963). The Washington, D. C., chapter of Gambler's Anonymous may be contacted through P.O. Box 4678, Washington, D. C.

come to Gambler's Anonymous for help, but help is needed for them as well.

Again let us repeat, not all who gamble socially are compulsive gamblers. Bergler distinguished between the neurotic sucker-gambler, the gambler-racketeer of organized crime (who does not really gamble at all), and the so-called "harmless gambler" who plays for diversion or sociability. Fifty million Americans tend to gamble in a moderate way, perhaps illicitly but not obsessively. The danger is that the occasional gambler, like the social drinker, may be trapped by increasing losses or the need to rebuild his ego into habitual gambling. Many of the 50,000,000 may be potential recruits for the 7,000,000 compulsive gamblers.

Gambler's Anonymous has designed the following questionnaire so that truly compulsive gamblers may recognize the signs of their own addiction. Compulsive gamblers can answer at least seven of the following twenty questions in the affirmative, according to the experience of Gambler's Anonymous.[9]

1. Do you lose time from work due to gambling?
2. Is gambling making your home life unhappy?
3. Is gambling affecting your reputation?
4. Have you ever felt remorse after gambling?
5. Do you ever gamble to get money with which to pay debts or solve other financial problems?
6. Does gambling lessen your ambition or efficiency?
7. After losing, do you feel you must return as soon as possible and win back your losses?
8. When you win do you have a strong urge to return and win more?
9. Do you often gamble until your last dollar is gone?
10. Do you ever borrow to finance your gambling?

[9] See Cole and Margolius, *op. cit.*, p. 16.

11. Have you ever sold any of your belongings to finance gambling?

12. Are you reluctant to use "gambling money" for normal expenses?

13. Does gambling make you careless of your family's welfare?

14. Do you ever gamble longer than you planned?

15. Do you ever gamble to escape worry or trouble?

16. Have you ever committed, or considered committing, an illegal act to finance gambling?

17. Does gambling cause you to have difficulty in sleeping?

18. Do arguments, disappointments or frustrations create within you an urge to gamble?

19. Do you have an urge to celebrate any good fortune by a few hours of gambling?

20. Does gambling, especially winning, build up your ego?

For many gambling is truly an itching disease. They are laughing themselves to death. In the world of unreality the neurotic gambler seeks a solution to all his problems in the fall of a card or the turn of a wheel.

AN ENCHANTING WITCHERY

We have seen that gambling probably began in primitive religion as an attempt to divine the intentions of the gods. Civilized man increasingly rejected the symbols of religion. He could not throw off the innate necessity to know his standing with the universe. Is it friend or foe? So, under the debased coinage of necromacy, as Ludovici said, he continues his divination around the gambling tables of so-called enlightened modern society. For many people, perhaps all, gambling represents a primordial appeal to fate, to destiny, to the supernatural, for some clue of approval or disapproval, acceptance or rejection, salvation or damnation.

Theodore Reik, Freud's brilliant student and colleague, described gambling as a "kind of question addressed to destiny. It is a form of oracle which the modern psyche readily accepts, although this latent meaning does not become conscious." [10] Others have spoken of gambling as an "accentuation of life." It is as if all the experiences of hope and disappointment, ecstasy and despair, were telescoped into these fleeting moments of play. Harold Smith, Sr., of Harold's Club, Las Vegas, says, "I am the guy who throws the truth at the people."

The motivations of gambling may be interpreted as basically religious or magical. To the supernatural religion says, "Thy will be done." Magic says, "My will be done." Beneath the surface sophistication of modern man is a primitive and animistic desire to discern or control the fickleness of fate. When man does not give his allegiance to the one and only God and Father of our Lord Jesus Christ he inevitably moves toward some idolatrous liaison. Man is incurably religious.

CONCLUSION

The gambler's motives are mixed and are not wholly apparent to us. Maurice Maeterlinck, the Belgian writer, says that gambling is "the stay-at-home, squalid, imaginary, mechanical, anaemic, unlovely adventure of those who have never been able to encounter or create the real, necessary and salutary adventures of life itself." The gambler evades reality and makes the pleasure principle all.

He may, as John Cotton intimated, be motivated by a get-something-for-nothing attitude halfway between idleness and avarice. Many are sick, compulsive neurotics impaled on the twin horns of winning and losing, needing both and unable to stand either. Beneath all our games of chance may be seen the primitive animistic magic that would determine destiny, or the primordial religion

[10] "The Study on Dostoyevsky," *From Thirty Years with Freud* (New York: Farrar & Rinehart, Inc., 1940), p. 170.

which would wrest some fateful divine disclosure for the future. "Am I accepted or rejected by the universe?"

While gambling is clearly symptomatic of many below-the-surface social and psychological motivations, it is finally a cheat and a fraud. In the end it gives nothing for something; compounds neuroses with personal, family, and financial damage; and places man's confidence in a fantasy of probabilities rather than the true God of all.

5

THE QUESTION OF LEGALIZATION

"I'm not ashamed of our lottery!" said New Hampshire's Governor John W. King. "The attacks of the professional 'do-gooders' don't bother me." Then he tells us *the good he has done* in authorizing the first legal lottery in modern United States history. Governor King insists we cannot legislate morals. Yet moderate gambling is quite moral according to his point of view. Thus he felt justified in signing the legislation of gambling against a considerable opposition of his citizenry. The governor assumes the compulsive gambler will not be attracted by the slow pace of the New Hampshire sweepstakes. He is apparently unaware of the addict's lust for losing—and in such a lottery he would have ample opportunity. Governor King believes the "little people" have more common sense than to overindulge in the sweepstakes against overwhelming odds. Yet he admitted the low-income status of New Hampshire residents and left us to wonder who but the little people will buy his lottery tickets. Obviously out-of-state residents must help. Governor King said his state has been "bearing a cross of taxation unprecedented in history." A Boston columnist observed: "New Hampshire expects to share its cross with its neighbors."

The political reasons for the governor's actions are obvious— "tough taxes versus lottery." He concluded his rationalization with the hope that other states will join and justify the wisdom of his noble financial breakthrough:

New Hampshire has entered into an experiment. There are no guide-lines laid down for us. We know that other states are watching the results, because our financial problems are by no means unique. We were faced with a choice between compulsory taxation through the proven, but harsh, method of a sales tax, and voluntary taxation through the sweepstakes. We feel sure that the sweepstakes will produce the revenue we need; that it can be run without the encroachment of racketeers and *without encouraging the violation of any* laws; and that it will not corrupt our morals.

We have not chosen an easy way out. Our sweepstakes will require administration of the highest quality. However, I am confident that in a couple of years or so, when the results begin to come in, I will be saying what I say now—that, far from being ashamed of our sweepstakes, I am proud of it, and of the effect it will have on education in the state.[1]

THE CASE FOR LEGALIZED GAMBLING

The pressure is on. The steam pipes are banging and the radiators are heating for an increase of legalized gambling. On the defensive, Governor King puts the case for the moral righteousness of

[1] *This Week Magazine* (July 14, 1963), p. 12.

his cause. When charged with the age-old practice of governmental profiteering from the vices of his people, he replies by naming vice virtue. Advocates of government-sponsored gambling make the following pleas: The considerable number of foreign government-sponsored lotteries is cited as evidence of the possibilities here. Why let Americans send to the Irish Sweepstakes 15,000,000 dollars which never comes back? The lottery corruption in the history of this country merely points to the need for tighter governmental control. To bar public lotteries and other forms of gambling is to repeat the travesty of prohibition. The proponents would say: "Because some thought drinking (gambling) wicked, because some people are self-destructive drinkers (gamblers), we turned over the drinking (gambling) business to society-corrupting racketeers. Chronic drinkers (gamblers) could still find booze (action) at will. The only change was that liquor taxes (profits from gambling) went to crooks instead of to federal, local or state governments." [2]

Representative Paul A. Fino of New York has introduced bills into the last several Congresses for a national lottery. They have never got out of committee. As quoted by Bill Gold in the *Washington Post* he offers four basic reasons or rationalizations for putting the United States government into the gambling business:

1. "It is common knowledge that the inclination to gamble is an instinctive part of human nature. If people have to gamble, let's give the profits to the government rather than the racketeers," he says.

2. "A national lottery would strike a blow at organized crime."

3. "It would reduce unemployment." In Puerto Rico 6,000 agents and vendors are employed. Ambiguously, Fino also suggests that our post offices sell the lottery tickets to keep expenses down.

[2] "Pro & Con: Should We Have State-Run Lotteries?" *Reader's Digest* (August, 1963), p. 104.

4. "A national lottery would yield billions in revenue, lower taxes, increase government spending." Fino likes to point out the number of Latin American and European democracies which have lotteries. Only the Communist bloc and the United States frown on them.

Like Governor King, Fino dismisses those who disagree with him as "moralists," "hypocrites," "do-gooders," and "bluenoses."

Even the *New York Times* has entered the fray. Mayor Wagner has repeatedly asked the state legislature to authorize New York City to operate and tax off-track betting. In the revenue squeeze the *Times* posed the same question as Governor King: Shall we have taxed gambling or other taxes? The editor believes that New York state is not about to abolish pari-mutuel, taxed betting within race tracks and its 106,000,000 dollars in revenue from that source. Hence, why not be consistent and let the less affluent people gamble legally off the track—with state supervision and taxation? The argument from the viewpoint of consistency would really point to wide-open legalized gambling once any gambling is distinguished by state designation.

Alvin J. T. Zumbrun, Executive Director of the Maryland Crime Investigating Committee, is one of the few nationally recognized criminologists to go on record in favor of legalized gambling. As an official in a state government which gains extensive revenues from racetracks, he summarized the arguments in favor:

1. Almost every proposal to legalize gambling is advanced as a means to raise revenue, by taxing and licensing.

2. A licensing system facilitates the control of gambling.

3. Gambling is based on human impulse too universal and powerful to be eliminated by law.

4. Legalization removes the control of gambling from the hands of

criminals who, in turn, control some politicians and some police officials.

5. Licensing removes criminals from gambling rackets, and the possibility of gang warfare is greatly reduced.

6. Legalization eliminates official corruption because gamblers pay license fees to the government instead of bribery to public officials.[3]

The most obvious reasons for the support of legalized gambling by politicians and harassed law-enforcement officers are these: Some politicians, faced with the need for increased revenue, would prefer to cater to the vices of their people for tax income rather than face the possible ire of the voters over increased direct taxes; and some law-enforcement officials, aware of the bribery corruption within their own departments and seemingly unable to beat it, prefer to join the opposition.

The less obvious reasons in some cases are undoubtedly the payoffs direct and indirect from syndicated gambling interests. David Hume's suggestion that Maryland politicians are frequently indebted to the gamblers for campaign support was mentioned earlier.

THE CASE AGAINST LEGALIZED GAMBLING

Opposition to legalized gambling comes from churchmen to be sure, but it also comes from a great host of professional criminologists, politicians, economists, businessmen, and historians. Our historical study has shown that religious and governmental opposition to gambling is centuries old. Opposition to legalized gambling in this country came from the rank and file. Whole communities were finally sickened of the fraud and social damage resulting from even the best government-regulated gambling.

Governor King says his sweepstakes can be run "without en-

[3] "Maryland: A Law-Enforcement Dilemma," *The Annals of the American Academy of Political and Social Science* (May, 1963), p. 62.

couraging the violation of any laws." Already Methodist Bishop
James K. Mathews of Boston has noted the governor violating the
spirit of federal laws against the mailing and promotion of lottery
tickets. The governor has made suggestions to the residents of
other states on how they can evade the intent of the federal law.
Convinced that gambling is moral, New Hampshire officials will
work to subvert the anti-gambling legislation of the federal government.[4] Suppose all the other states enact lottery legislation to protect themselves against New Hampshire's siphoning of tax funds
across state lines. Imagine the prospect of all the states competing
with each other for such blood money to support their own causes.
Each state would have to give bigger prizes and better breaks to
woo suckers from neighboring states. America would become known
for its free competition in the encouragement of the get-something-
for-nothing attitude.

Congressman Fino's four arguments for a national lottery have
been ably answered by Bill Gold, columnist for the *Washington
Post.*

1. Against the "instinctive" argument, Gold says the urge to
punch one's boss in the nose, to steal, to lie, and to murder are
equally widespread. Civilized adults have developed a moral self-
control which curbs these impulses. They expect their governments
to do the same. In effect, he is saying that we *must* legislate morals
—indeed, all legislation has its moral aspect. Will our legislation
represent a civilized, grown-up morality or a return to the bush?

2. In a card game with friends, says Gold, the group tends to
check each individual's tendency toward extravagance which would
transform "a minor vice into a major calamity. But the loser who

[4] See "Needed: Counteraction Against Lottery," *The Christian Century* (May
22, 1963), p. 668.

wants to 'get even' by doubling his bets in a commercial gambling enterprise finds the house eager to accommodate him."

3. If anti-gambling laws are being enforced the compulsive player may not be able to find the action he wants—even with friends. Hence, he may have to hold on to his money in spite of himself.

4. "It is nonsense to argue that we ought to put the Government into the gambling business because this would create new jobs and bring in a lot of revenue from a vice that laws are powerless to stamp out. You could use the same 'reasons' to advocate legalizing marijuana or prostitution." [5]

Fino fails to mention the large percentages taken off the top by foreign lotteries, greatly increasing the odds for the citizenry. Figures on the top ten foreign lotteries indicate they are no assurance for reduced taxes. Lotteries abroad rarely produce, in net income, over 2 per cent of total government revenue—in most cases less than 1 per cent.[6]

Virgil Peterson replies to the argument from consistency advocated by the *New York Times* and others. The poorer classes have never been able to have all the privileges of the wealthier groups, he says. Why should we want to guarantee the "have nots" the same opportunity to gamble away their meager funds with the largess of the "haves."

For Mayor Wagner's proposal the *Times* would do better to wear the same editorial face exhibited for Mayor O'Dwyer's proposal to legalize bookmaking on sports events. A decade ago a *New York Times* editorial entitled "A Way to Spread Gambling" rejected Mayor O'Dwyer's plea: "Once the principle of legal gambling on

[5] "The District Line—Lottery Bill's Logic is Underwhelming" (March 11, 1963).
[6] *This Week, op. cit.,* p. 6.

the street corners is endorsed, there is no stopping place . . . that there would be a great deal more gambling than now, we believe cannot be denied. . . . We cannot endorse a solution that would, in the end, only mean more misery for people who already have hardships enough." [7] The Kefauver Committee Report on Organized Crime concurs with the *Times'* earlier position: "The operation of handbooks and other gambling establishments in places that are easily accessible to the working man and the non-habitual bettor results in the spread of the evils of gambling to increasingly larger segments of the population." Milton G. Rector, director of the National Council on Crime and Delinquency, and New York Supreme Court Justice Samuel H. Hofstadter rejected Mayor Wagner's proposal. Mr. Rector told the *Christian Science Monitor,* "such a system would increase gambling, tax the poor, sweeten the take of the racketeers, and aggravate the city's perennial problems of corruption, narcotics, and prostitution." [8]

The major arguments against legalized gambling are:

1. *Legal gambling contributes to illegal gambling.* Quotations from the Massachusetts Crime Commission have already shown the effects of pari-mutuel's camel nose in the tent. Illegal off-track betting has grown from nothing to a monstrous, syndicated "something" since the legalization of race-track gambling in the thirties. The income from the state is not worth the cost of increased law enforcement and welfare.

2. *The licensing of gambling establishments is no guarantee of keeping the criminals out.* Licensing is invariably a political matter, administered by politicians in terms of political debts to be repaid. How can we expect the very officials subject to bribery by gamblers

[7] January 11, 1950.

[8] Emilie Tavel, "Off-Track Bets and Crime" (December 27, 1963), p. 1. See also "Judge Says Off-Track Betting Opens Crime Door" (December 28, 1963), p. 3c.

to suddenly become circumspect when called upon to administer a licensing system.

As Kefauver pointed out, racketeers are attracted to gambling, not by its legal status, but its huge sums of easy money. Racketeers have entered all kinds of legitimate business—trade unions, juke boxes, recordings, sports, labor unions—if they thought there was a way to make big money under the guise of respectability. Profits can then be reinvested in vice operations. Gambling gold, not legal status, is the honey which attracts the racketeer bees.

3. *Anti-gambling laws can hardly be compared to America's experiment with national prohibition of alcoholic beverages.* Anti-gambling laws are nearly all local in nature. The federal government does not try to tell the farmer in Missouri and the lawyer in San Francisco what he cannot do in the privacy of his own home. Gambling laws do not prohibit private and social gambling itself. Rather, they are directed against the business of gambling devoted to profit on the weakness of the people. Prohibition dealt with a product the sale and possession of which is easier to control than gambling. The gambler sells no product but avarice—a hope, a fascination, a lust to have something for nothing. As a control system even the licensing of liquor has been faulty and fraudulent since 1933. The licensing of a lust—like prostitution or gambling—is even more difficult to control. Enforcement is always lax.

4. *Legalized gambling demoralizes the government (the built-in winner) as well as the poor people (the built-in losers) it victimizes.* By concentrating on bleeding its citizenry's weakness, it does not assume obligations of fiscal responsibility. Latin America's heavy dependence on lotteries, says the *Los Angeles Times*, "has mischievously delayed the day of effective and equitable finance." Harlan E. Atherton, superintendent of schools in Concord, New Hampshire, troubled by his state's new lottery for education, said,

84

"I take a dim view of subjecting education to the vagaries of voluntary contributions." Police Chief William H. Parker of Los Angeles said, "Any society that bases its financial structure on the weaknesses of its people doesn't deserve to survive."

5. *Legalized gambling educates people to gamble.* Great Britain has found out that wide-open legalization does not control, but encourages gambling. "We are in the grip of a gambling fever," said the Reverend Kenneth Greet of the Department of Christian Citizenship of the British Methodist Church. Whether it be the state, or even churches, which sponsor gambling activities they contribute a *respectability by recognition.*

Public agencies whip up the enthusiasm to gamble. Gerald Ellison, the Bishop of Chester, described this to the Churches' Council on Gambling meeting in London. The government-chartered British Broadcasting Corporation encourages gambling by providing "irritating and dreary information about betting and tips," he said.

Legalization and all its promotion softens the community for illegal gambling. Thus the respectable overworld condones the criminal underworld, contributes to a lack of public morality, and a general indifference to laws, courts, and police.

It is significant that opposition to governmental gambling comes most strongly from independent crime commissions, outstanding newspapers and networks, and leading politicians and law-enforcement officers, as well as many churchmen. Virgil Peterson, operating director of the Chicago Crime Commission, has written the most outstanding book against legalized gambling. Aaron Kohn, director of the New Orleans' Metropolitan Crime Commission, and Dwight S. Strong, director for the New England Citizens' Crime Commission, have both voiced their strong opposition.

In January, 1950, Thomas E. Dewey, governor of New York, addressed his legislature concerning Mayor O'Dwyer's request for legalized betting on sports events. Recalling his earlier experience as the district attorney who prosecuted the "Dutch" Schultz gang gambling bribery case, he said:

The entire history of legalized gambling in this country and abroad shows that it has brought nothing but poverty, crime and corruption, demoralization of moral and ethical standards, and ultimately a lower living standard and misery for all the people.

I am unalterable opposed to the proposal which has been made by the Mayor of the City of New York.[9]

Former President Harry S. Truman has made clear his opposition to legalized gambling. Count Cavour, the George Washington of modern Italy spoke of state lotteries as a "tax on imbeciles."

To the warnings of the *Los Angeles Times*, the *Detroit News*, the *Christian Science Monitor*, and most of the New Hampshire papers, Chet Huntley of NBC news recently added another. Huntley stressed economic, political, and moral arguments against legalized gambling. In the area of economic drawbacks, he stated that gambling prevents commercial growth and keeps industry out. Money is taken out of the hands of consumers, and most of the profits on gambling—far in excess of revenues—go out of the state. Family tourists are discouraged. Nevada is an unhappy example of all of these.[10]

No newspaper has been stronger in its opposition to gambling than the *Washington Post*. It has waged war on Maryland slot machines close to home and on New York bingo as well:

New York's bingo law has worked about the way laws to license and regulate gambling usually work. A State inquiry has found that

[9] *The Annals of the American Academy of Political and Social Science* (May, 1950), p. 38.
[10] NBC White Paper, "The Business of Gambling" (April 28, 1963).

the professional promoters who operated before the law continued their operations. The chairman of the inquiry sadly concludes that "it is difficult to predict whether this area of legalized gambling will ever be successfully administered and enforced."

It is, on the contrary, easy to predict that it will not be successfully enforced. The only wise government attitude toward gambling is one of hostility. Licensed or unlicensed gambling exerts a corrupting influence upon everything it touches. It corrupts those engaged in it commercially. It corrupts those who are supposed to regulate it. It corrupts the public by spreading, like an infection, the passion to get something for nothing. Perhaps the State cannot stop it altogether; but at least it does not have to join the gamblers in a conspiracy to subvert citizens and government alike.[11]

CONCLUSION

Recognizing the high costs of government and the politician's difficult task of finding revenues, we must encourage realistic and responsible state financing. Political support must be given to wise increases in fair tax plans for adequate support of necessary public welfare. Politicians must be dissuaded from vote-getting gambling shortcuts which avoid fiscal responsibility.

Law-enforcement officers must not be allowed to argue the case for enforcement upon the difficulty of enforcement and the presence of corruption. There have been times in nearly every American city's history when prostitution, racketeering, murder, robbery, and burglary should have been licensed if resistance and corruption were justification for legalization. We must ask, "Will licensing reduce to a minimum the evils that attend the enforcement of existing prohibitory statues without creating new ones that are even more objectionable?"

Ray H. Everett, Executive Secretary, Social Hygiene Society of

[11] Editorial (January 16, 1962).

the District of Columbia, has stated, "After all the evidence is in, we may well conclude that legalized prostitution does not have a logical leg to stand on . . . good laws and vigilant enforcement may not eliminate commercialized prostitution, but they can keep it down to a minimum." What is said of prostitution is equally applicable to commercialized gambling.

6

SHAKEDOWN OR STEWARDSHIP

"The dubious gains of petty gambling are not acceptable in financing the work of the church. All Methodist churches shall abstain from the use of raffles, lotteries, and games of chance for church support or church-related projects." [1]

Most all the religious groups in America stand together in their opposition to gambling in any form. They would support the above-stated position of The Methodist Church against gambling as a money-raising device within the church or synagogue. The one major exception to this united stand against gambling is the Roman Catholic Church. Conflict between the Roman church and other religious groups is often prominent when legalized gambling is put

[1] *Doctrines and Discipline of The Methodist Church*, 1960, ¶ 2022.2.

before a local community or state. It is important that Americans understand the positions of the churches and synagogal associations on this important issue. Churchmen should certainly be familiar with the position of their own denomination.

THE ROMAN CATHOLIC POSITION

Actually there is no official position of the Roman Catholic Church on gambling; that is, there is no papal dogma or encyclical on the subject. No church council has delivered itself on the subject in recent years. Early church councils and fathers were adamant against gambling on the part of Christians. During the modern period, however—certainly since the Council of Trent—the Roman church's attitude on the subject has considerably moderated. Today the matter is approached simply as a moral question. Catholic moralists agree that gambling in itself is not intrinsically evil. The Archdiocese of Washington, D. C., furnishes us with the Roman Catholic moral attitude in the following quotations from a book of questions and answers on Roman teaching and morals:

To play games of skill like golf or chess, or games of pure chance like poker or black-jack for a stake, is not in itself sinful. I may lawfully spend my money for recreation, and give my neighbor some of it, if they prove more skillful or more lucky than myself. A game of poker becomes of interest only when some stake is in sight for the winners. Gambling becomes sinful, if we force a person to play against his will, if we cheat, if we stake money not of our own, or use money needed for our debts or for the support of our families.

Betting also is not sinful in itself, if the event at issue is really uncertain, if both parties understand the bet in the same way, and if both are prepared to pay if they lose.

But all Catholic moralists are agreed that gambling and betting may lead to grave abuse and sin, especially when they are prompted by mere gain. The gambler usually frequents bad company, wastes much valuable time, becomes adverse to hard work, is strongly tempted to be dishonest when luck is against him, and often brings financial ruin upon himself and those dependent upon him.[2]

In other words, Roman Catholics see no inherent evil in gambling itself. It is not sinful in principle, although it may be sinful by reason of motive or circumstance.

A prominent Roman Catholic book, *Moral and Pastoral Theology* by Henry Davis, S. J., continues the above line of reasoning. If there be no abuse or corruption lotteries are thoroughly consistent with justice and the law of nature. They may be used by the state, by the church, and by individuals for financial income. Father Davis expressed some concern that the individual "should not derive a greater personal profit from a lottery than if he had put his money into a successful business." [3]

Father Davis does admit, however, that "lotteries are dangerous transactions, for they induce people to buy beyond their means, they foster cupidity and avarice, and even, in the simple, encourage superstition and magic." He warned against repeated lotteries and all the variations of the same—sweepstakes, coupon competitions, missing word competitions. These encourage a spirit of gambling and nurture avarice. State lotteries encourage such a wanton, wasteful spirit. They should be kept within very narrow limits, he said.

In some areas the Roman Catholic Church has conducted casino-like gambling operations within parish houses for church financial support. Bingo is a more frequent parish operation. Roman Catholics with the encouragement of their church have worked hard

[2] Bertrand L. Conway, *The Question Box* (New York: The Paulist Press), p. 277.
[3] New York: Sheed and Ward, Inc., 1958, p. 404-6.

for the legalization of such gambling as the bingo games for charitable purposes in the state of New York.

A Protestant pastor from Hot Springs, Arkansas, wrote:

No Protestant Church, to my knowledge, has accepted gifts or favors from the gambling interests, unless you would so construe the personal financial support of a church member whose livelihood comes from one phase or another of the "business." The Roman Catholic Church regularly holds Bingo Parties and Benefits in one or another of the casinos. They have had no part, so far as I know, in protesting even the illegality. The Bingo itself, conducted by the church, is in violation of the law, even when held in the Parish House of the Church.

In some cases Roman Catholic churches have conducted such operations in open violation of state laws against such gambling. Law-enforcement officers are thus put in the quandary of "winking" at the law violated by the church—and if by the church, perhaps many others—or of strictly enforcing it. Dwight S. Strong of the New England Citizens' Crime Commission insisted that the church's illegal gambling softened up the people for all sorts of illegal gambling outside the church. "One Boston church," he said, "displayed six automobiles and attractive young women at a sidewalk booth selling chances at the time the Attorney-General of the Commonwealth was a member of this church." [4]

When "CBS Reports" presented "Biography of a Bookie Joint" showing the close connection between illegal gambling and members of the Boston police force Cardinal Cushing demanded a public apology to the city of Boston. This was shortly after the Cardinal had declared to a Boston Police Ball, "In my theology, gambling itself is not a sin any more than to take a glass of beer or of hard

---

[4] "New England: The Refined Yankee," *The Annals of the American Academy of Political and Social Science* (May, 1963), p. 43.

liquor is a sin." Perhaps the Cardinal is one of those who look upon gambling graft from the underworld as a peccadillo part of the game, since gambling should not be illegal in the first place. If public officials accept payoffs at this point, where is the cutoff? Once gambling be defined as innocent in *principle,* will there be so much concern over admittedly evil *consequences* associated with gambling? The *Reporter* magazine commented on the Cardinal's compromise, and all on churches whose moral witness may have been blurred by a willingness to let the most worthy Christian ends justify the most dubious financial means: "Apparently it is left for mass communications, those reporters who serve it best, and playwrights, to awaken the public conscience."

In all fairness it should be admitted that some Roman Catholic officials have forbade gambling among their people. Catholic bishops opposed the slot machines in the Maryland legislative fight against them. Cardinal Meyer of Chicago called for the discontinuance of bingo games in Roman Catholic parishes when this practice was defined as illegal by the city. His concern was that Roman Catholics obey the law and cooperate with law-enforcement officials. Many parishes have turned to the stewardship principle of tithing rather than the shakedown principle of gambling as a means of church support.

THE NATIONAL COUNCIL OF CHURCHES

In the midst of the 1951 Kefauver Committee hearings in Congress the General Board of the National Council passed a resolution on "Gambling and Public Morals." It reaffirmed the vigorous opposition of its member churches to gambling "as an insidious menace both to personal character and social morality." Churchmen were called upon to reject gambling in every form and strongly support strict enforcement of gambling laws. An examination of existing laws was called for, so that new measures might be adopted for more adequate prosecution where necessary. The churches were reminded of their primary responsibility to educate and activate the necessary moral concerns of their members. Succeeding general boards and assemblies have reiterated this position. This position was renewed by the General Assembly in 1963, and a national seminar was planned to organize the church's opposition to legalized gambling.

The two denominations in America who consider themselves as much participant in the Catholic tradition as Roman Catholicism, the Protestant Episcopal Church (Anglican) and the Greek Orthodox Church, have spoken their opposition to gambling.

1. *Anglican position.* The Lambeth Conference of 1948, representing Anglicans (Episcopalians) all over the world, passed the following resolution on gambling:

The Conference draws attention to the grave moral and social evils that have arisen in many lands through the prevalence of gambling on a vast scale. In view of these evils we urge that no Church organization should make money by gambling. We depreciate the raising of money by the State or by any organization through sweepstakes and similar methods, however good may be the object for which the money is raised; and we warn men and women of the danger of acquiring the habit of gambling, which has led in so many cases to the deterioration of character and the ruin of homes.

One of the best statements on the moral character of gambling was made by the late Archbishop of Canterbury, William Temple. He argues that gambling is not necessarily a practice springing directly from an evil character. Nonetheless, it is wrong in principle. It is inherently evil, though the evil immediately involved in mod-

94

erate and self-controlled gambling is very small. The distribution of money by chance is a socially wrong principle. "Wealth ought to be distributed in accordance with (a) need; (b) service rendered; (c) service expected; the last is the justification of inherited wealth." [5]

Gambling—the distribution of money by chance—is not only wrong in principle, but by consequence it is a source of immense moral and social evil. The moral man cannot repudiate responsibility for his influence on others, on society. *Against the Roman Catholic position, gambling is wrong in principle and consequence as well.* No doubt the amount of harm present in a small bet cast by someone who could easily afford it would by itself be negligible. Yet if the action on a wide scale causes desperate havoc to multitudes of people it becomes the clear duty of Christians to resist the fundamental principle.

2. *The Orthodox position.* The Greek Orthodox Church of North and South America has made no official pronouncement on gambling. However, the Biennial Clergy-Laity Congresses of the Church have expressed themselves opposed to gambling in any form. Churches are forbidden to hold any games of chance on their premises or at any church-sponsored activities.

Churches having no official position on gambling but possessing an understood "common code" against gambling in any form are the United Church of Christ and the Disciples of Christ. "The American Lutheran Church has not taken an official position with respect to the question of gambling," according to its secretary, William Larsen.

1. *The Evangelical United Brethren Church,* now considering

[5] "Gambling and Ethics," an address given to the Church Assembly, autumn, 1932, p. 8.

union with The Methodist Church, says to its members: "The gambling 'craze' is a menace to society, destructive of good government and deadly to the best interests of moral, social and spiritual life. All members of the church are expected to abstain from gambling in any form." [6]

2. *The United Presbyterian Church* has taken an especially strong stand against gambling in any form. Criticism is addressed against the principle of "getting something for nothing" inherent in gambling, as well as the devastating moral and social consequences that accompany it. Legalized gambling is opposed. "No good cause can be promoted by a practice so evil. No person or community is so rich as to be able to afford the resulting deterioration of personal integrity, the poor work habits, the demoralization of family life, the unchristian attempt to get something for nothing or at another's expense. No legislation can make lawful in the eyes of God or before man a practice so immoral." [7]

Earlier, in 1952, the General Assembly of the United Presbyterian Church had said:

It is our conviction that "big time" syndicate controlled gambling grows out of "small time" gambling. By participating in games of chance and wagers at bridge and golf games the Christian conscience may be dulled and powers of reason laid aside. Therefore—

1. We call on all church members to avoid taking part in any kind of gambling, even for charitable causes.

2. We urge church members to acquaint themselves with local and state laws regulating gambling practices.

3. We oppose all efforts to legalize gambling, and call upon sessions and presbyteries to do likewise, since it is contrary to Christian principles to seek public gain by exploiting human weakness.

[6] *The Discipline of the Evangelical United Brethren Church, 1955,* ¶ 1911.
[7] The General Assembly of 1954.

4. We commend those citizens who have organized to bring about the elimination of corruption born of the alignment of gamblers and public officials.

United Presbyterians also brand "lotteries and bingo games in churches as particularly reprehensible, even though justified by law" (1954 General Assembly).

3. Henry Kolbe has studied the official General Conference statements of *The Methodist Church* on gambling since unification in 1939.[8] Due to the moral lapse and increased gambling of the war years, he finds a gradual strengthening of the Methodist position in the successive *Disciplines*. In 1952 a statement urging abstinence from gambling within the church was included. In 1960 the statement was strengthened to read: "No lottery, raffle, or other game of chance shall be used in raising money for any purpose" (¶ 272). This change represents the church's concern about the encroachments of a gambling culture on its own life.

Elsewhere in the *Discipline* of 1960 we find the church's concern about the social and moral consequences of gambling upon the world outside the church. In the Methodist Social Creed, the church expresses its concern to "aid the individual, the home, and society to overcome the social, economic, and moral wastes which accompany . . . gambling in any form" (¶ 2020, IIIC). An additional statement of the 1960 General Conference on gambling is found in *The Discipline*:

The passion to acquire wealth without honest labor, inflamed by widely publicized giveaway programs and the growing movement to legalize gambling in state after state, is a serious concern for Christians. The practice of gambling undermines basic moral law as well

[8] See "Gambling and the Church," an Adult Fellowship Series reprint from *Adult Student* and *Adult Teacher* (September, 1961), pp. 19 ff.

as established economic laws. Gambling is a menace to business integrity, breeds crime, and is destructive of the interests of good government. (¶ 2022.2.)

The Board of Christian Social Concerns of The Methodist Church has urged stricter law enforcement of anti-gambling laws and rejection of legal recognition by the state. New approaches for rehabilitation of compulsive gamblers should be undertaken by church and state alike. Local churches are asked to educate and motivate members to decision and action against gambling, legal and illegal. The churches must foster the spiritual and mental health, the moral integrity which can withstand the cultural coercions to gamble. Christians who find their adequacy in God and their joy in the welfare of others need no such artificial crutch for their lives.

Roger Burgess, Associate General Secretary of the Board of Christian Social Concerns, told the story of another Methodist pronouncement on gambling.[9] We have previously noted the new legislation in Maryland to outlaw slot machines in four southern counties. Contributing to this victory was the crusading effort of Protestant and Catholic ministers and laymen. The organizational meeting of this opposition was called by Bishop John Wesley Lord at the Methodist Building in Washington, D. C. To this group Bishop Lord, chairman of the Division of Temperance and General Welfare of the Methodist Board of Christian Social Concerns, said:

Religion and morality are the indispensable supports of political and national prosperity. To strengthen and not subvert these great pillars of human welfare is the supreme duty of every patriotic citizen. A nation's greatness can always be measured in terms of its virtue.

[9] *Ibid.,* pp. 49 ff.

The slot machine is an evil in our midst which strengthens and demonstrates the communist charge that we are a morally undisciplined and spiritually depraved people. For a government, be it federal, state or local, or for any other agency, however worthy, to finance itself out of the weakness of the people is abhorrent to right-minded persons, and serves the cause of the enemy.

When we give our support to or tolerate the slot machine menace, we subvert our historic American creed and wield the communist sickle. America is no stronger than the ideals of her people.[10]

OTHER DENOMINATIONS

The Assemblies of God counsel members to avoid gambling in any form, including lotteries. They encourage abstinence in lands such as El Salvador, which has a national lottery, as well as the United States. The Church of the Nazarene and the Conservative Baptist Association of America define their opposition to gambling in terms of a purity and morality of life required of genuine Christian discipleship. Though having no official position, The Southern Baptist Convention issues pamphlets calling for abstinence and opposition to all legalization measures.

Literature of the Jehovah's Witnesses calls upon those who "love what is righteous and upbuilding" to abhor gambling. Seventh day Adventists say, "We do not countenance gambling because we believe that the money which comes into our hands is a sacred trust and should be used for God's cause and purposes."

DeWitt John, Manager of the Committees on Publications for Christian Science headquarters in Boston, wrote:

The Church of Christ, Scientist, does not condone gambling even in its mildest, unorganized, or amateur forms. It considers gambling an evil which is inconsistent with the practice of our religion. We believe

[10] *Ibid.*

gambling has a degenerative effect on character, places an unnatural emphasis on chance, encourages a dangerous hope of getting something for nothing, and throws true, lasting values out of perspective.

In its more aggressive, commercialized forms, gambling becomes a major social problem, magnifying these undesirable effects many times, especially in its frequent alliance with organized crime. Legalizing gambling in the form of national or state lotteries or sweepstakes simply compounds the problem, since experience has shown that gambling begets gambling, and legal gambling by no means eliminates illegal gambling or the fraudulent and vicious influences which surround this activity.

For a government to exploit the moral weakness of its citizens as a source of revenue seems to us to be entirely unjustified on any grounds.

THE JEWISH POSITION

Representing Conservative Judaism, the United Synagogue of America has ardently opposed the legalization of bingo games for charitable purposes in New York state. Believing that the raising of funds for synagogue or charitable purposes is itself an act of sanctity, they oppose all gambling methods for such purposes. The means of fund raising must have the same spiritual quality as the ends to which the funds are to be employed. United synagogues are prohibited from such activity even though sanctioned by civil law. In 1960 a Brooklyn congregation was expelled from this association for noncompliance. Other synagogues are under investigation and have been warned.

Orthodox Judaism concurs with this position: "The employment of religious auspices or religious premises for the operation of gambling enterprises is a *chillul Hashem,* a desecration and perversion of religious life." [11]

[11] *Jewish Life* (September-October, 1964), p. 5.

CONCLUSION

The moral and theological discussion of gambling will be continued in the following chapter.

It would appear that the position of religious groups on the gambling question is closely related to their economic ethic, and fund-raising practice. Roman Catholicism is willing to advocate the social distribution or extraction of wealth by chance as a principle and practice. Since this was not the early principle and practice of the church, one cannot help believing that a decay in practice has led the church to justify in principle a type of financial support from which it cannot, or will not, extricate itself. The pressure of practice upon principle—of means upon ends—is clearly illustrated in the 1961 quotation from a British Roman Catholic bishop. "It is always a great sorrow to me that we have to use such undignified means of raising money as bingo and the pools. But let us make it clear that we shall use these methods—and even more undignified ones—so long as they are this side of honesty and so long as we need the money for our schools." [12]

Judaism insists that means must be consistent with ends. With this Anglicans, Orthodox, Protestants, and Evangelicals will agree. The use of money—getting, spending, giving—is a sacred matter for the Judeo-Christian tradition. Life and its material possessions are a stewardship granted by God to man. We are responsible to God in the use of all our money, in the sacrificial way we use it to support God's church and the needs of our fellows. The faithful and grateful giving of money to the church or charity—without thought of monetary reward—is as important for Christian growth to giver as to the receiver.

Gambling by the church for church profit is no more than a

[12] "Gambling Since 1960," *Annual Review of the Churches' Council on Gambling* (London, December 31, 1962), p. 44.

"shakedown" of people who would not give for the love of God or man unless so tempted by materialistic prizes and rewards. The church's using such methods encourages a materialism in the use of money that is as vicious as that of Communism and is completely contradictory to Christian stewardship. The end is corrupted by the means.

Especially reprehensible is the religious group which gambles in open violation of the civil law. The church or charity thus becomes a part of that respectable *overworld which condones the criminal underworld* in its activities. The gambling church condoning gambling in principle softens and educates the community for the outlaw "oddsmakers."

7

NO "CHANCE" FOR THE CHRISTIAN

William Temple, late Archbishop of Canterbury, testified before the British Royal Commission on Lotteries and Betting in 1933:

Gambling challenges that view of life which the Christian Church exists to uphold and extend. Its glorification of mere chance is a denial of the Divine order of nature. To risk money haphazard is to disregard the insistence of the Church in every age of living faith that possessions are a trust, and that men must account to God for their use. The persistent appeal to covetousness is fundamentally opposed to the unselfishness which was taught by Jesus Christ and by the New Testament as a whole. The attempt (inseparable from gambling) to make profit out of the inevitable loss and possible suffering of others is the antithesis of that love of one's neighbor on which our Lord insisted.[1]

Let us examine Temple's argument in detail.

A DENIAL OF THE DIVINE ORDER

In a recent Lenten devotional book the preacher took as his text the words of the soldiers at the Crucifixion: "Let us not tear it [Christ's robe], but cast lots for it to see whose it shall be." The author then read into the text his own curious view of life as a gamble. For him Jesus Christ is the chief gambler, calling upon us to gamble for his kingdom. Such theological confusion is hardly worthy of the pulpit or publication.

Life is not a gamble. It is not a chancy game for the Christian. God is in control.

> This is my Father's world,
> O let me ne'er forget
> That though the wrong seems oft so strong,
> God is the Ruler yet.

The Christian rejects fate, kismet, or lady luck as a basic principle of reality. We worship no goddess of chance, the lady Tyche.

God's kingdom, his ultimate victory, is not up for grabs. It does not primarily depend upon *our* gamble, our hazarding of life for him. The conclusive victory for God's reign over the universe has already been won by Jesus the Christ. The fulfillment of that reign, incorporating all our response, will be finally secured by him.

Faith is not a risk, as some existentialist theologians suggest, a leap into the impossible, the unknown, the absurd. To be sure, we walk by faith rather than sight in this life, but faith provides us

[1] William Temple, "Gambling and Ethics," issued by The Churches' Committee on Gambling, 215 Abbey House, London S. W. 1, England, p. 15.

with another kind of knowledge and a personal assurance which is just as certain as the additional kinds of sense knowledge we gain from sight. "Faith is the substance of things hoped for, the evidence of things not seen" (Heb. 11:1 K.J.V.,) or as the R.S.V. has it, "faith is the assurance of things hoped for, the conviction of things not seen." Not seen, tasted, touched, heard; but evidence, assurance, conviction, nevertheless—here is the unshakeable conviction of the Christian life that "God loves me and forgives me and abides with me for evermore."

> How firm a foundation, ye saints of the Lord,
> Is laid for your faith in His excellent word!
> What more can He say than to you He hath said,
> To you who for refuge to Jesus have fled?
>
> "Fear not, I am with thee; O be not dismayed,
>   For I am thy God, and will still give thee aid.
> .   .   .   .
> The soul that on Jesus still leans for repose,
> I will not, I will not desert to his foes;
> That soul, though all hell should endeavor to shake,
> I'll never, no, never, no, never forsake!"

This faith of ours is no risky leap in the dark. God is our sure foundation, our mighty fortress.

Gambling is bad theology. As William Temple put it, "Gambling challenges that view of life which the Christian Church exists to uphold and extend. Its glorification of mere chance is a denial of the Divine order of nature." Just as gambling arose out of primitive religious attempts to divine or control the will of the gods, so it continues today, stripped of its theological symbolism, as a religious (or magical) rival of the Christian faith. The Christian rejects luck and chance and looks to God for the final purpose of life and the direction toward these purposes. Understanding the universe as a purposeful, consistent creation, the Christian takes the odds of life and transforms them in response to the will of God. Lives dedicated to the whim and caprice of chance and luck deny the providence of God. A Christian cannot conscientiously do this.

There is a risk in the Christian life, however. It is the risk of what we may be required to give up for that one and only security —Jesus Christ and his kingdom. Christ and his kingdom are a certainty. The risk is in the taking up of our crosses to follow him. To follow the King of love who rules from a cross we must be prepared to suffer and sacrifice. "Blessed are those who are persecuted for righteousness' sake, for theirs is the kingdom of heaven . . . for so men persecuted the prophets who were before you." (Matt. 5:10, 12.) This is no ultimate risk, however. The certainty of Christ and his kingdom is the only abiding certainty. When twentieth-century America has settled in the dust of the pharaohs Christ and his kingdom will abide.

> Only one life, t'will soon be past.
> Only what's done for Christ will last.

The greatest loser of all—the real gambler against whom all the odds are stacked—is the fool who wins the whole world and loses his own soul.

DISREGARD POSSESSIONS AS TRUST

The Christian concept of stewardship before God involves time, talents, possessions, and self. Our Lord's parable of the talents (or use of money) is well known to us. God expects us to invest ourselves and our possessions wisely with imagination and industry that they may show good social use and an adequate increase (Matthew 25:14 ff.). We are not so familiar with the Master's definition of the steward as the trusty and sensible man who is found at his task, making wise and sober use of his responsibilities at all times (Luke 12:42 ff.). While a man may be a proprietor over property in relation to his fellow man, he is a steward in his relation to God. He holds all things in trust from God, accountable to him finally for their use. He is not free to do as he likes with what God has given him in trust.

In eighteenth-century England John Wesley, the founder of Methodism, argued that the beverage alcohol industry was immoral because it diverted good grain from the mouths of the hungry. It was not a responsible use of God's resources. On stewardship principles Wesley believed that all property and possessions are given in abundance by God for the welfare of all. After our needs and those of our family are adequately met all excess should be devoted to the welfare of others.

Wealth ought to be distributed according to (1) need, (2) service rendered, (3) service expected, argued Archbishop Temple. "No one proposes that wealth should be distributed in accordance with chance. That is a false principle . . . exceedingly active to the great hurt of individuals and of society; therefore it ought to be altogether repudiated." [2]

Bad economics is bad ethics. The Christian use of money surely works toward the elimination of poverty and a more equitable distribution of wealth among all God's children. Gambling works to effect exactly the opposite. It would make the unthinking many poorer for the profit of the undeserving few. The two triangles be-

[2] *Ibid.*, p. 8.

low illustrate how gambling puts a reverse into Christian social and economic progress:

<table>
<tr><td>CHRISTIAN
ECONOMIC PROGRESS</td><td>GAMBLING</td></tr>
</table>

The privileged few

The undeserving few
(winners and promoters)

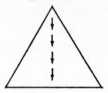 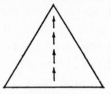

The less privileged many   The unthinking many (losers)

In one case the movement is a redistribution from the few to the many resulting from an enlightened social conscience. It is based on justice, need, reason, and religion—Christian stewardship. In the other case the money passes from the many millions to the few, the big winners and promoters, and none of these factors enters into the transfer. It is based merely on greed and chance. The gambling regression is indefensible socially and morally.[3]

Gambling is a violation of the principles of Christian stewardship. "To risk money haphazard is to disregard the insistence of the Church in every age of living faith that possessions are a trust, and that men must account to God for their use." The use of possessions in God's account must surely be for the welfare of the many rather than the few. No one should be more interested than the Christian Church in society's responsible stewardship of its resources unto God. What kind of Christian stewardship is it when a church encourages the gifts of the community for turkey dinners, bazaar

[3] See J. Clark Gibson, "Gambling and Citizenship," a Beckly pamphlet, 4th series, (London: Epworth Press, 1956), pp. 6-7.

bric-a-brac, fish pond and bingo prizes, rather than for the love of God and neighbor?

APPEAL TO COVETOUSNESS

Covetousness or greed is considered sinful throughout the Bible. The *excessive* desire to have something for oneself or to have more than one already possesses and needs is a subject of commandment and warning throughout the Old and New Testaments. Jeremiah regarded the greediness of his people as a principal cause of their decline and exile (6:13; 8:10; 22:17). Our Lord counseled, "Beware! Be on your guard against greed of every kind, for even when a man has more than enough, his wealth does not give him life" (Luke 12:15 N.E.B.). The Apostle Paul equated "ruthless greed" with fornication as sins to be avoided (Eph. 5:3).

In some passages covetousness or greed is identified with idolatry. "The greed which makes an idol of gain" has no share in the kingdom of Christ and of God (Eph. 5:5). Ruthless greed is nothing less than idolatry (Col. 3:5). Where a man's treasure is, said our Lord, there is his heart; he who loves material possessions cannot truly love God (Matt. 6:21; Mark 7:21-23; Luke 12:15; cf. Rom. 1:29).

In the gambler's pantheon of gods "mammon" must be added to "chance." Covetousness or greed is the high priest of this pagan temple. Such idolatry has no place in the Christian life; it is self-destructive in any life. "No one can serve two masters; for either he will hate the one and love the other, or he will be devoted to the one and despise the other. You cannot serve God and mammon (Matt. 6:24). "But seek ye first the kingdom of God and his righteousness . . ." (Matt. 6:33 K.J.V.). The Christian teaching at this point is clear; equally clear is gambling's elevation of materialism and covetousness to an idolatrous place of priority. "The persistent appeal to covetousness is fundamentally opposed to the unselfishness which was taught by Jesus Christ and by the New Testament as a whole."

PROFIT FROM OTHER'S PAIN

"You shall love your neighbor as yourself." Love for neighbor is another major theme in the Christian life. Such neighbor regarding concern is derived and dependent upon the love God has shown *for* us in Christ and *in* us by the Holy Spirit. Christian love from God through us to neighbor is not merit seeking, but merit creating; not self-protecting, but self-giving. It is universal in its concern for all men, but capable of particular application to individuals. Christian love is essentially a relationship expressed between individual persons, but the Christian is also concerned for the crowd. The Christian's willingness to work for social justice is a manifestation of love for his neighbors in the crowd, those near and far whom he may not know personally.

The sacredness of personality proceeds from God's love for all. All men are *not* created equal in their native ability, their inherited position, or their social potential. All men *are* equally recipients of God's love, however. Thus every person is of sacred worth to the Christian. A Christian will not use another person as a means for his own gain, nor will he be content while others practice this in society. A Christian will treat all men as precious in God's sight.

Gambling is wrong because it violates Christian love and concern for others, the sacredness and dignity of human personality. Gambling is a pleasure and profit gained at the cost of other's pain and loss. Because the gambling operator uses the individual as a tool for his own profit, gambling is an immoral act against the sacred dignity of man. The common term for the customer is "sucker." Gambling uses (manipulates) persons as means to a selfish end. It may be argued that the loser is rewarded by the excitement of the game. All too often this is not true.

110

Gambling is also destructive of personality because it tends toward excess. The compulsive gambler is as sick a personality as the alcoholic. Anything which hurts or stifles the normal growth of the human personality is morally wrong. Since gambling psychologically depresses the creative faculties, shortcuts honest labor, and undermines the fulfillment of vocation, it is wrong.

The strongest case against gambling arises when one considers the total impact upon society. The billions thrown into the quicksands of gambling and used to finance the vice syndicates of the nation could be used for food, housing, education, or religious needs. Gambling is a parasite on the business community, a foremost inducer to embezzlement, an inviter to poverty, and a perverter of family life. The state or the church which seeks to finance its worthwhile ends by means of encouraging and legitimizing the weakness of its people contributes to the degradation of society. The get-something-for-nothing attitude undermines the integrity, industry, and creativity of a people.

Gambling is morally wrong because of its damaging effects upon persons and society. "The attempt (inseparable from gambling) to make profit out of the inevitable loss and possible suffering of others is the antithesis of that love of one's neighbor on which our Lord insisted."

MODERATION OR ABSTINENCE

The moderate gambler will probably say that he does no harm with his gambling, and if others do harm with theirs that is no affair of his. This kind of ethical individualism (relativism)—antisocial in character—is damnable from a Christian point of view. Perhaps the attitude is even worse than the negligible damage done by the moderate gambler. To say he doesn't care two bits about his neighbor, about his influence upon society for good or ill, is to retreat from responsible maturity to an infantile self-centeredness. The moral man (the moral society) is a responsible man (society), responsible to God for self and others. Irresponsibility is man's abdication of his humanity. We are made to be moral, decision-making creatures.

The decision to ignore one's own influence with regard to gambling is akin to shouting "fire" in a crowded theater. Though the deed may assert one's rights, it ignores his responsibilities. It may affirm his freedom, but it is falsely purchased at the expense of his duties. "To repudiate responsibility for one's influence is as profoundly wicked as anything can be—far wickeder than most crimes of passion—for it denies one of the springs of all obligation." [4]

Here again Christian love recognizes the social nature and responsibilities of the self. "You shall love your neighbor as yourself." "If, when you are bringing your gift to the altar, you suddenly remember that your brother has a grievance against you, leave your gift where it is before the altar. First go and make your peace with your brother, and only then come back and offer your gift." (Matt. 5:23-24 N.E.B.) Paul said: "Let us therefore cease judging one another, but rather make this simple judgement: that no obstacle or stumbling-block be placed in a brother's way" (Rom. 14:13 N.E.B.). He did not call for an end to the ethical evaluation of others' deeds; he asked that we not take the place of God, who alone has the right of ultimate blessing and cursing. Rather, let us remain in fellowship with all men insofar as humanly possible. Because we love all those for whom Christ died we intend to put no obstacle in any man's way. We will not add our influence to the climate of permissive gambling which encourages the childish and the compulsive, the corrupt and the criminal.

Actually the "golden mean," the ethic of moderation in all things, is not Christian. It comes from a pagan, Greek heritage which

[4] Temple, *op. cit.*, p. 9.

stresses the rational balance between extremes. Unfortunately Roman Catholics have perpetuated much of this emphasis introduced into medieval moral theology by the rediscovery of Aristotle. At best "the golden mean" could be applied only to the morally good. Moderation in evil is absurd as a moral standard.

Thus one is still faced with the necessity of defining good and evil. Christianity knows the good to be God whose nature of sacrificial love is expressed in Jesus Christ. "Not too much" is a pale and anemic substitute for "Take up your cross and follow me." Following the Christ, cooperating with his Holy Spirit, means the sacrifice of self-interest for the sake of others. It means standing up to be counted when human values are at stake, denying yourself pursuits which may lead to the hurt of persons and the harm of a society.

Whenever a pursuit may be said to have an evil motivation (greed), a wrong principle (chance distribution of wealth), and antisocial consequences (crime, corruption, compulsion, economic waste) for the moral man, for the Christian, abstinence is the best policy. Gambling is such a pursuit demanding abstinence.

CONCLUSION: A CHRISTIAN RESOLUTION

The Christian is unable to submit his life to any other priority and providence than that found in the God and Father of our Lord Jesus Christ. There is no "chance" for the Christian. He accepts time, talent, and treasure as a trust from God to be used for his glory and for the welfare of all his children. His love of neighbor stands against every practice which harms the growth of the human spirit toward the likeness of Christ or breaks down the structures of justice in society.

Therefore, the Christian will refrain from the private practice and the public endorsement of gambling in any form, realizing that gambling is detrimental to the purpose of life as defined in Jesus Christ.

8

FAITHFUL STEWARDS
OF MANIFOLD GIFTS

A Prayer for the Deliverance of Society
from the Misuse of Money

Almighty God, who dost require of all men that they should be
faithful stewards of thy manifold gifts: We beseech thee that in
getting and spending we may not misuse our stewardship. Deliver us
from the selfishness that seeks gain without labor, or excitement without care for its cost to others. Set free those who are possessed by the
gambling spirit and break the power of those who exploit their weakness. Prosper the efforts of all who are striving to remove the evils
of betting and gambling and lead all men to seek in Thee their true
joy and to find in Thy service the fullness of life; through Jesus Christ
our Lord. Amen.[1]

[1] J. Clark Gibson, "Gambling and Citizenship," A Beckly pamphlet, 4th
series, No. 1 (London: Epworth Press, 1956), p. 10.

What can the churches of America do to oppose the gambling mania—legal and illegal? (In many cases churches and synagogues will stand together against this menace.)

RETHINK AND TEACH PRIORITIES

There is a serious need upon us for rethinking our goals and values in terms of the Christian faith and way. As churchmen, gathered in worship and study, scattered in witness and service, we need to re-examine our system of priorities.

1. *The God and Father of our Lord Jesus Christ must be acknowledged as the ultimate creator, judge, and redeemer of our lives.* "You shall love the Lord your God with all your heart, . . . soul, and . . . mind" is the commandment of Christ. God is first to be loved, obeyed, and served. This leaves no place for greed, no priority for success, no primary concern for wealth and fame. Our Lord Jesus Christ attacked the worship of mammon, whether money or materialism.

This contagious idolatry begins in the home where little children are infected by their parents. Do our children perceive their primary goal in life to be material success, or do they most of all want to please God and serve their fellow man? Is success so important to our children that they will seek it at the expense of integrity? Are we numbered among the hard-eyed bargainers that afflict our civilization, to whom nothing is precious but only profitable? If so, how can we expect our children to be otherwise? Certainly the pressure on our homes from the outside will be tremendous, but Christian parents can exert the greatest influence their children will ever receive, the moral suasion and godly devotion of a Christian home.

Take away the worship of mammon in our homes, even in our churches, and we will greatly inhibit the get-something-for-nothing attitude. This is best done by receiving and acknowledging something else first in the place of mammon: "I am the Lord your God. . . . You shall have no other gods before me."

2. *We need to review radically our Christian understanding of work.* Of course work can become drudgery and so much tedious exertion. Some who extol the virtues of work just for the sake of work have never tried it. There is a very real sense, however, in which God calls all of us to a necessary work in his world in which he continues the constant work of his creation. God calls everyone of us to work at a job which is needful and, thus, sustains the good life of our fellow men. A Christian should not be employed in a job which does not serve the genuine needs of humanity.

Likewise God calls each of us to a job which will develop the talents and abilities that he has placed within us. If Jesus' parable of the talents means anything it means that he holds us responsible for developing our personal gifts. How else can we become what we are meant to be? God calls us to a job that will help him in ordering the communal life of all mankind. God needs some of us to raise food for humanity, but not all of us. God needs some of us to build more attractive and efficient homes for humanity, but not all of us. In the heavenly father's providential ordering of life there is a place for each of us.

Our society must take seriously the need to provide purposeful jobs for all our people. Unemployment is a serious threat to personhood as well as to our economy. Every man needs to work; every man deserves a share in the fruit of his labor. "Something for something" is good economics and good ethics.

3. *The third priority for renewal is the Christian doctrine of money.* The economic question is crucial to the nation. With all the resources God has given how shall we cut the economic pie? How shall we distribute the wealth of raw material, soil fertility, and climate; of industry, imagination, and work; among capitalist,

laborer, and consumer? Does the earth belong to the conquerors, to the conquered, or to neither—only to the Lord? If to the Lord, how shall we use this trust for him for the welfare of all?

God's economics is Christian stewardship. The church teaches this but seldom with daring and conviction. No area in American life has been more consistently evaded by Christian ethics than economics. This is partly due to the almost closed mind of Americans with regard to economic alternatives to the sacred cow of capitalism and free enterprise. Christians in other lands—for example, Methodists from Scandinavia and England—have asked that the American churches give more consideration to the socialist criticism of capitalism. Actually the Christian Church, in the wisdom of its centuries under many systems, knows that no economic system is thoroughly consistent with Christian stewardship. The churches must be actively engaged in the testing of all systems and the teaching of God's economics.

For the Christian money is never an end in itself. It is "coined personality" representing the life and labor of a man to be used in the service of God and humanity. It must not be stolen, for thus we deprive others of part of their personality, their life and labor. Even stealing by mutual consent—gambling—is wrong for what it does to the persons involved. It is a false principle for the distribution of wealth. Its motivation is not the service of humanity. Its economic consequence is a paralysis of business enterprise, a cornering of the consumer's dollar for questionable ends.

As long as "I wanta get rich" is the primary motivation of Western man, the church must continue to tell the parable of the rich fool who built bigger and better barns and lost his own soul. "What kind of fool am I?" Some will even be required to sell all that they have and give to the poor in order to follow the Christ down the crowded ways of modern life. The joy of life is in the sacrificial service of him who moves among the stables and shops, through the open fields and crowded tenements of human need. Our money and possessions can be used to sustain ourselves and all those Christ seeks to serve.

4. *The fourth priority for renewal is the Christian doctrine of community.* The church's theology of individual motivation is pretty clear, but our theology of society is rather fuzzy. Hook, line, and sinker we generally swallow the "ragged" individualism so much a part of American culture without examining whether it be biblical or Christian. Consequently we tend to lay all the burden of accomplishment and success upon the individual. "The plunder belongs to the strong and the gifted," we say. "Give the public what they want instead of what they need."

"Horatio Alger" lays a heavy burden upon the average and less-than-average citizen of a technological society. Confronted by economic and political problems too big to handle and unable to pull himself out of the urban mire by his own boot straps, he readily resorts to gambling and crime as a possible way out.

The biblical understanding of individual-in-community and the social nature of the self must be given more attention in the church's teaching of Christian ethics. Society or the government is not an impersonal "they" to be fought and limited for the sake of sacred individualism. Rather, the individual finds fulfillment of himself in relationship with other individuals in community, society—a government "of the people, by the people, for the people."

Government representing all the people must be encouraged by the church, with Christians participating therein to serve the common good, the welfare of all. This will include laws and enforcement restraining the vicious inclinations of man as well as enabling acts and programs to enhance his health, education, and welfare. Ways must be found for society to assume a responsible role of love and care for all its members. Purposeful employment; playgrounds and educational opportunities for the young; better housing, food, and medical care—all these are the concerns of a responsible society for its citizens, and all these can contribute to the fullness and security of people so that crime, gambling, alcoholic beverages, and narcotics are no longer needed as the companions of insecurity and despair.

Of course the Christian faith knows that such social engineering and stage setting cannot provide the ultimate answers for man's incurable God-sickness deep down. But the doctor must frequently treat the festering symptoms on the surface before he can heal the source of the problem within.

Thus we see that the churches must assume a greater responsibility for thinking and teaching basic Christian ethics in pulpit and pew. New ways must be found to scatter the Christian ethic abroad throughout the decision-making centers of our society. New forms of ministry will be developed to accomplish this among various vocational groups—none neglectful of the geographical and home-based ministry of the local parish.

ASSUME CHRISTIAN CITIZENSHIP RESPONSIBILITIES

1. *The church must support stronger anti-gambling laws and enforcement.* In most states commercialized gambling is clearly illegal. The late Senator Estes Kefauver and Attorney General Robert Kennedy have led the fight for stricter controls on gambling to assist the states against this syndicated interstate criminal enterprise. In the face of extensive graft and payoff in local law-enforcement circles such strong federal laws and action are sorely needed. Under the laws enacted in 1962 prohibiting interstate transportation of gambling paraphernalia, information, and promotion, many of the wire services and bookie joints closed shop. In the first thirteen months after the laws were passed the FBI looked into 4,990 pos-

sible violations. Of these, 943 cases were forwarded to the Justice Department for further study; 115 persons were indicted and 26 convicted the first year.

Such laws and enforcement can be supported and encouraged in every community of the land. Study the federal legislation and the laws of your own state concerning gambling. Find out the facts about gambling in your own state and community. Inform others.

Encourage support for good law enforcement and express opposition when laws and enforcement are lax. Write letters to the editor. Get acquainted with local officials of the courts and police department. Let them, and state officials as well, know of your concern about this issue.

Write your governor and ask for his help in establishing an independent commission to study organized gambling in your state. Such commissions can lead the way to more effective legislation and enforcement. Suggest a mayor's conference on gambling.

Support candidates who will work for tougher laws and stricter enforcement.

Sponsor a research seminar on "gambling and law enforcement" inviting public officials, legislators, the attorney general, et cetera, with as much press coverage as possible.

Strive for interfaith consensus against gambling through a clergy conference for the community.

Refuse to take part in sweepstakes and give-away contests. Write the sponsoring companies challenging them to lower prices instead of engaging in publicity-minded give-away contests.

Report your opposition to law-enforcement officials if charity, civic, or fraternal organizations engage in illegal raffles or bingo.

Anyone engaged in professional gambling (bookies especially) should be reported to the Internal Revenue Service. By federal law they are required to register and pay a fifty-dollar permit to gamble.

Also every gambling device must have a federal gambling stamp (250 dollars) on it. Some cities and states where gambling is illegal have made the possession of such federal permits prima facie evidence of law violation. Encourage such a position in your community. Write for a list of the gambling stamps issued in your state and report this to proper state and local authorities.

Such responsible support of legislative and law-enforcement agencies by an awakened citizenry is gravely needed.

2. *The church must work against legalized gambling.* In spite of all the glamour of Hollywood entertainment, the free transportation to Las Vegas and return, "the sinister truth," according to reporter Fred Cook, "is that Nevada's legalization of gambling was one of the greatest boons ever bestowed on the American underworld by a grateful government. . . . The net result has been to make 'fun-loving' Las Vegas virtually the capital of American crime." [2] Churchmen need not be apologetic and timid about fighting such an adversary as this, though other churchmen, veterans' organizations, and charity dupes may unwisely be in the forefront of the opposition.

The kind of open discussion and exposure of the nature of local gambling and its operation suggested under number one will help prepare the climate for community opposition to legalized gambling.

Be prepared to answer the "sportsmen" who want to slip in pari-mutuel betting for the sake of improving horses. Don't let them forget what it does to human beings. Watch the "humanitarians" who want gambling revenues for education and welfare.

Let your Congressmen know of your opposition to any form of national or state lottery.

Organize channels of communication and action through annual

[2] "Gambling, Inc," *The Nation* (October 22, 1960), pp. 298, 301. See also Lloyd Shearer, "Gangsters, Gambling, Girls, and Show Business," *Parade: The Sunday News-Press* (January 12, 1964).

conferences, presbyteries, or state conventions which can be quickly pressed into service against sudden pro-gambling legislation. Councils of churches, state Christian civic foundations, ministerial associations, and other groups will help.

Prepare church members for the crisis by a sustained training in Christian ethics. Why it is wrong to gamble should be made clear for every Christian.

To offset the appeal for gambling revenues the church should encourage an adequate and wise tax basis for state services. Churchmen will want to do this anyway out of concern for the health, education, and welfare of the whole citizenry. Fiscal responsibility is a necessary prerequisite to adequate governmental services on the local and state level. Don't let "penny wise and pound foolish" tax conservatives back your state government into gambling for quickie revenues. Churchmen should support higher wages and qualifications for policemen as a check against the spoilers and grafters. Be willing to pay the bill—out of Christian concern.

3. *The church must support rehabilitation programs for compulsive gamblers at the local, state, and national levels.* If Karl Menninger can rate 7,000,000 alcoholics one of our most serious health problems in America, surely compulsive gambling is not far behind. The 4 to 6,000,000 gambling addicts in the United States comprise a serious mental health problem. Through the Yale School of Alcohol Studies and other agencies there has been a gradual increase in state and local councils devoted to the study and treatment of alcoholism. The public has profited by the information disseminated by these agencies.

This has yet to be done in the equally acute moral sickness of compulsive gambling. As with alcoholism, the healing therapies of the church, medicine, and psychiatry have been of little help. The group therapy of Gambler's Anonymous has proved helpful in a small number of cases. New ways of help and healing must be found. The churches should seek these ways to help the gambler in their own redemptive fellowship. They should also encourage the research and rehabilitation programs of all state and private agencies consistent with Christian concern.

4. *The church must encourage community-wide, long-term education on gambling for youth.* Certainly those states who finance themselves by encouraging this weakness of their citizens have an obligation here. Why should they not inform the citizens of the odds against them in the government sponsored games? Cigarettes may be required to indicate the harmful effects of their use upon the package. Why should the state not want to protect its citizens from the harmful effects of gambling?

Even in states where gambling is illegal public education on the subject would greatly aid in the fight against criminal gambling—the supporting indulgence of the two-dollar bettor and the fifty-cents numbers player. High-school courses on good citizenship should include material on gambling problems and the need for law obedience and enforcement. This would be a natural association with information on traffic safety and the use of alcoholic beverages. Of course the churches must not expect the schools to teach their particular Christian position for abstinence or moderation. The facts can be presented, however, and encouragement to individual commitment be made. Attention can be given to various church positions as a matter of information. Certainly the state and local agencies of education would want to encourage the obedience of all anti-gambling laws.

An annual debate topic on the question of legalized gambling in the 1950's served such an educational purpose.[3]

[3] *University Debater's Annual, 1950-51,* edited by Ruth Ulman (New York: The H. W. Wilson Company, 1951).

Again, there is no substitute for the church's own sustained training in Christian ethics for her own members.

FULFILL THE CHURCH'S MAIN MISSION

The church must lead its own people through education and commitment to newness and wholeness of life in the Spirit. The mature Christian finds his joyful acceptance in the God and Father of our Lord Jesus Christ. In this supreme security the Holy Spirit works to deliver Christians from the materialism of Mammon, the frenetic thrills of Baachus, the eroticism of Venus, the crushing conformity of Demos, and the chancy temptations of Tychus. In this community of the Spirit personal and social habits such as gambling should be openly discussed without intimidation by the sophisticated libertine or the self-righteous pharisee. When youth and adults are acquainted with the facts they should be allowed the freedom of the Spirit to make their own behavioral commitment in terms of their own personal appropriation of the love of Christ. A new life in Christ supplied by all the resources of God's gracious Spirit will become increasingly dissatisfied with the cardboard crutches and plastic flowers of contemporary paganism. The church's preeminent task is to be the agency, the nucleus of this healed and healing new humanity which finds its adequacy in God and its success in the welfare of others.

Grant, O Lord, that we be faithful stewards of thy manifold gifts —especially this new life and community we have from thee. "Happy that servant who is found at his task when his master comes!" (Luke 12:42 N.E.B.)

INDEX

125